Je remercie ici Janine Weill
de sa précieuse collaboration
de disciple et d'ami. Merci amie

Marguerite Long

at the piano with
FAURÉ

by Marguerite Long

Translated by Olive Senior-Ellis

KAHN & AVERILL, LONDON

First published by Kahn & Averill in 1981
This paperback edition first published in 1996 by
Kahn & Averill
9 Harrington Road, London SW7 3ES

British Library Cataloguing in Publication Data
A catalogue record for this book is available from the British Library

ISBN 1 871082 60 9

Printed in Great Britain by
Halstan & Co Ltd., Amersham, Bucks

contents

1 Meeting

It was a sweltering afternoon in August, 1902. An unusual liveliness animated the château of Comte de V . . . , a distinguished amateur musician. The piano, which had been tuned the previous day, was waiting to be opened, while four music stands stood back-to-back, ready for a quartet.

What a beautiful château Mireval was, standing reflected in a mirror of water at the bottom of the park. Below the steps, on the gravel drive, carriages, drawn by high-spirited horses, were pouring out their occupants. The cream of society was there, all the charm of the period displayed in its elegance.

The programme handed to each arrival announced that the host and his friends were to hear a Brahms quartet. The courteous invitation extended to me, my sister Claire and her husband, who was then Commander of the garrison in the ancient city of Castelnaudary, was not entirely disinterested: I was accustomed to be asked to "play something" and was accordingly prepared. I had already become less than fond of this salon atmosphere since attentive listeners are rare and the comments of the connoisseurs given with a well-informed air so as to appear original.

Comte de V . . . called for silence from his audience and the first part of this private concert had passed pleasurably when the host came and asked me to play. I was at the start of my career and my title of *Premier Prix du Conservatoire de Paris* retained all its prestige in this charming and distant province. That, at least, was what I said to myself as I went

1

to the piano in a silence prompted as much by curiosity as by sympathy. I have kept one of my portraits of that period and my appearance in those days amuses me now. Could anyone take seriously this fragile young girl whose pale, fuzzy hair kept escaping from an ineffectively coiled chignon in uncontrolled whisps, and whose turned-up nose seemed to be sniffing at the wind?

I launched into Beethoven's *Thirty-two Variations in C Minor*, followed by Liszt's *Polonaise in E*. These were received with great enthusiasm. Since I was satisfied with my performance, I was about to grant the audience some degree of understanding when my host approached, smiling. After showering me with elaborate compliments, he conveyed a message from a young officer present who asked "would I be so kind as to play now one of the piano pieces of Gabriel Fauré".

I was aghast. I knew Gabriel Fauré by name, just as I had heard of some of his works, but I had never played a note of them. To my great embarrassment, I had to admit my ignorance. Afterwards I learned that this "herald" of Fauré refused to be presented to me and kept repeating querulously: "I don't understand your enthusiasm for this young girl. She plays the piano very well, but she's no musician if she can't play any Fauré."

The future was to change his opinion and give me my revenge. Three years later I started playing Fauré; and I married that young man.

It was in this way that a remark casually tossed into the air was to have a decisive influence on my life. I had indeed been a bit annoyed at having to refuse the young stranger's invitation to play some Fauré, but in fact I was hardly to blame. At the beginning of this century Fauré's music did not feature in the piano repertoire. Only his songs could be heard in the few salons frequented by music enthusiasts, those of the Marquise de Saint-Paul, Madeleine Lemaire and the Princess de Polignac, among others.

Although the music often sparkled there, incompetence often gave rise to some charming blunders. And little has changed since. Not long ago, at a musical reception given by the Duchesse of X . . ., the lady of the house swept me into one of the rooms where, apparently, people were asking for me, and said, in all innocence: "Here she is, the Queen of the Violin!" Needless to say, I had difficulty in suppressing a burst of laughter. Another amusing comment, just as true, is worth recording. It was made by a lady of the high aristocracy who, after hearing Franck's *Sonata*, declared: "I really do prefer it with orchestra!"

By an odd co-incidence, all the people who were to fill my life, for better or for worse, I had met at the one time during the preceding summer.

In 1900 the grand première of Gabriel Fauré's *Prométhée*, commissioned for the amphitheatre at Béziers by the patron of the arts, Castelbon de Beauxhostes, on the advice of Camille Saint-Saëns, was spoiled by the weather. A storm of unusual violence had broken over the town and was followed by three days of torrential rain. Could this have been a belated echo of the Anger of the Gods towards the man who stole the Fire of Heaven to offer it to mankind? The management of the amphitheatre decided to repeat the performance the following summer. My sister and brother-in-law, with whom I always spent my holidays, had brought me with them to hear *Prométhée*. A carnival atmosphere reigned in the town. After the performance, musicians, actors and spectators wandered through the streets or took refreshments on the terraces of the pavement cafes.

One group stood out. The composer of *Prométhée*, wearing his little white boater jauntily over one ear, seemed to be paying marked attention to a very pretty young woman who was the master's latest fancy. This lady was a pianist and, well, ambitious, and she had just filled the place left vacant in Fauré's rather flighty heart. The master, attractive, cajoling — in a word, adorable — possessed to a supreme degree the art of disentanglement with a disarming lack of self-consciousness. It had become second nature, and made him prefer flight to explanation. It was an unconscious unreliability, perhaps, but one which he practised in friendship as in love. My first hearing of the grandiose *Prométhée* that day in Béziers did not arouse in me any wish to investigate further the music to which my artistic life was subsequently to be so closely tied. The idea of being presented to the composer did not even cross my mind.

I have already said elsewhere what the threads of my destiny were. My happy childhood at Nîmes, with gentle and understanding parents, was filled with music. My sister, who was eight years older than I was, had worked with a teacher of German origin who was called Mager and who had gained Premier Prix in Antoine Marmontel's class at the Paris Conservatoire and had been a fellow-pupil of Francis Planté. He had already realised the benefits of a synthesis of the French and German teaching methods. It was my sister who directed my piano studies. I studied at the Lycée and the Conservatoire at the same time where, after a competition and still very young, my sister had been appointed to a teaching post. I worked well, although often rebelling against the discipline she tried to impose on me. I was unquestionably gifted and adopted the habit of reading while practising Hanon's exercises for hours on end. Perhaps that is where the secret of my supple fingers lies!

Music for me wasn't just those hours I spent at the piano; it was every kind of music. I knew by heart, and could sing, entire scores. I loved improvising transcriptions and paraphrases *à la manière de Liszt*. My tastes were those of the day: *Aida*, *Les Huguenots* delighted me. I gave so many imaginary recitals! I can still see myself playing for hours and hours in front of an imaginary audience. The illusion was so strong that I felt transported by happiness. A premonition? Perhaps . . . My vocation had already been made clear in a real concert in the Grand Théâtre at Nîmes. Dressed in pink and wearing small white shoes with rosettes, I played Mozart's *Concerto in D minor*. It was on that day that I felt I was being called . . .

Nevertheless, at the age of thirteen I was frightened by the prospects that a new life in Paris opened before me. I was aware of what I would have to leave behind to pay the price. There would be no more dazzling bullfights. I loved "my" arenas, with the crowd, thirty thousand strong, squeezed onto its slopes, vibrating with the same uneasy feelings. I had the soul of an aficionado: those sparkling costumes, the Moment of Truth, the skilful passes of the muleta held no secrets for me. My only real punishment would be to be deprived of going to the bullfight. When I think of it, it still makes my heart beat faster. And I still regret having been deprived of the horse races that the Spanish government was to have offered me if, as I so much wished, I had been able to go to Madrid to receive the decoration of *Commandeur d'Isabelle la Catholique,* which, apart from the great honour it brings, also allows one, I am told, the privilege of going into church on horseback. Once again, I was being punished . . . And I was having to leave all this and face my destiny alone and go into a convent! What kind of life would this be for me? Very hard, deprived of the gentleness that growing children need, no sun . . .

Théodore Dubois, who was then Inspector of Music at the Beaux-Arts, had been checking on my musical abilities for two consecutive years and they had been marked by rapid progress. He came to see my parents, urging them to send me to Paris. He did not hesitate to declare that "this little girl will be a great virtuoso". My mother, who was already ill, was worried at the prospect of seeing me so young and alone in the capital, free to indulge the in-born laziness with which I would readily have kept faith! Although I had not yet heard of it, I shared the humorous viewpoint of Tristan Bernard, who held that "work is not meant for man since it tires him!" The change in our domestic situation troubled my mother greatly, and she would depress herself by saying:

"These poor little girls will have to go out and work now."

At that time Paris seemed like a distant mirage, one of those lofty places you dream about without thinking you'll ever get there. To tell the truth, I hardly gave it a thought and was quite happy with the imaginary life that gave me so much pleasure. Once I had arrived there I immersed myself in music and worked at my studies, drawing my sole consolation from them. The only times I went out were when I visited an uncle who didn't even have a piano. When I was at his house I worked on the table and in this way I learned Bach's *Fourth Prelude and Fugue* by heart!

Nonetheless, in two years I had cleared all the obstacles presented by the competitions of the Conservatoire, passing on all levels: preparatory and superior, in a single season, and obtaining my Premier Prix at the first attempt. Successively, I was the pupil of Mme Chéné, whose colleague I was to become fifteen years later, and of Henri Fissot, who was an exceptional teacher. He instilled in me that feeling for the quality of sound which later became one of the touchstones of my teaching. This success — almost too swift, as the award of my prize had just confirmed — had so overwhelmed me that on the evening of the competition I burst into tears when the results were announced. Mixed with my joy was the memory of my mother who had just died. Ambroise Thomas, who was Director of the Conservatoire at the time, noticed this childish grief as he left the judges' room, leaned towards me and said: "You mustn't cry, my child. You'll get your reward next year." He hadn't recognised me, and this unexpected consolation renewed my tears, and yet I smiled at my good fortune.

Indeed, a very pleasant life was opening before me. Although, before making certain of my career, for some years I enjoyed the amenities of a wordly life with a degree of pleasure, going from ball to ball, leading the cotillions, horse-riding, even skating until one day when I witnessed an accident that cost a young skater the use of two fingers, and I recognised the danger of this sport to my career.

I had been adopted as one of the family by Mme Garnier-Gentilhomme who ran one of the best-attended French classes in Paris at that time, and I taught the piano to one of her sons, preparing him for the Conservatoire.[1] To tell the truth, I didn't like teaching, for I hadn't yet felt the joys of this fine profession. Nevertheless, and despite all the trappings of a marvellous life, I began to feel its emptiness. Music presented itself to me rather flatteringly, but rather vainly, too.

I became the favourite player of some charming musicians. Benjamin Godard, Francis Thomé and Théodore Lack composed some sparkling pieces for me which displayed all the facility and brilliance of my technique . . . but still I felt dissatisfied. It seemed that they thought of me as the pianist who could do justice to their music, and I felt isolated among them. The single exception was Antonin Marmontel who wrote a piano waltz, *L'Enchanteresse,* that I often played. One day when I was feeling depressed, I went to see him to ask his advice: "Can you get me to do any work?" I felt an untapped energy inside me which I didn't know how to channel. He was delighted that I had regained my conscience and my clear-sightedness. Touched by my trust, he blushed with pleasure and agreed to instruct me. For many years from that time I spent all my Sunday afternoons with him, in his studio in the Rue Blanche, working on all the classical and romantic repertoire, benefitting from the thorough study of a work, learning to acquire the patience to "put the work on the piano for the hundredth time". In a word, Antonin Marmontel showed me the beauty of teaching — these were the finest years of my apprenticeship.

Antonin was the son of the great Antoine Marmontel, who had taught Louis Diémer and Francis Planté, among others, and was one of the most sought-after teachers in Paris. He used to have his lunch brought in to him without interrupting the lesson, eating a mouthful here and there, and sometimes

[1] Georges Garnier abandoned music for poetry. He died tragically.

popping a chip or a piece of fruit into the mouth of his pupil! Albert Lavignac tells the story of how his parents had managed, with great difficulty, to arrange a meeting with the famous teacher "at six o'clock". All spruced up, his hair specially curled, and with a lace collar topping his velvet jacket, the child prodigy had turned up at Marmontel's where he was greeted with much ill-feeling. Marmontel said to him: "What have you come to do at this time of day? It was at six o'clock *this morning* that I was expecting you!"

Although I wanted to, I never was lucky enough to meet him. One day when I had played particularly well, my teacher decided to have me play for his famous father, and the occasion was arranged for a certain Tuesday. At the said hour I duly went to the Rue de Calais and asked the concièrge which floor I should go to. "There's no point in going up, Mademoiselle. You won't be let in." I insisted, of course, explaining that I was expected. Same refusal. "But, really, Madame, since I've told you that I have an appointment, why won't you let me go up?" "Why not?" she answered, "Because M. Marmentel died this morning."

Thereafter I often went back to the Rue de Calais, and I well remember, among the many lovely paintings decorating the flat, the Greuze portrait of Glück, as well as the fine Delacroix painting of Chopin (now in the Louvre) under whose gaze I have often played the works of the Polish genius.

It was during the course of one of those Sunday afternoons that my teacher advised me to work on the music of Gabriel Fauré. He chose the *Third Valse-Caprice*. "As soon as you're ready, I'll ask him to listen to you." I was attracted to it at once and felt that my supple fingers would find a new lease of life in the music. Isn't it odd that this happened just after I got back from Mireval? The work was quite unknown to me. It was composed in 1891 for the pleasure of "female ears". I worked hard at the piece and grew to love it more with every passing day. Sustained by my enthusiasm, I didn't allow myself to be taken aback by the difficulties of Fauré's piano writing, and my interest was retained by the originality of the music. Eventually the day arrived which was to be the date of our first meeting. When I crossed the threshold of his house in the Boulevard Malesherbes, my heart was thumping furiously. Fauré greeted me with the kindness and simplicity that were so characteristic of him. He was fifty-eight then, but he did not show it. (Saint-Saëns used to say of him: "Gabriel Fauré has no age, and never will have.") I remember clearly the emotion that gripped me. I was worried, but transported with joy; agitated, but beaming. And for the first time I was "at the piano with Gabriel Fauré". I played the *Third Valse-Caprice*. Fauré listened attentively, doubtless himself worried at this first contact with the young girl who was to play his music. Did he realise from the first how eager I was? Was he aware of the sister-soul beating beneath the fingers of this young musician? Did he feel that a human being, instinctively grasping the hidden meaning of his music, was preparing to plunge herself into his work, to make it known and understood?

When I had finished, Fauré seemed so pleased that I was both rewarded and enthralled. He had the *Sixth Barcarolle* on the piano, and he entrusted it to me, asking me to work on it. I left, very proud, with the work under my arm and a promise to come back soon. I did not go back to the Boulevard Malesherbes that Spring, but from that day on I entered wholeheartedly into the music of Gabriel Fauré.

2 *Testimonies*

It was chance that brought me to the master again in that summer of 1903 at Aix-les-Bains, which at that period was the main centre of musical activity during the summer and was renowned for its theatres and concerts. All the great artists could be heard there. I had been engaged for some concerts of chamber music and for an orchestral concert at the Casino. I was to play the Schumann *Concerto* under the baton of Léon Jehin who was Director of Music at the Monte Carlo Theatre during the winter. He was an excellent conductor as well as a musician of sound judgement, outstanding at Monte Carlo where he gave the premières of some of the masterpieces of the budding century — notably Gabriel Fauré's *Pénélope,* before the work's Paris performances at the Théâtre des Champs-Elysées in 1913.

When I arrived at Aix, I was delighted to see a poster announcing a concert of music by Fauré, to be performed under the direction of the composer. When we met he asked about my work and suggested that I play him the Schumann Concerto and his own *Sixth Barcarolle* which had been with me all the while. There was so much I could learn about music from such a teacher! Unlike Chopin and Debussy, who played their own music as no orther mortal could hope to, Fauré was not a virtuoso, nor even a player of any great skill, but to hear him play taught me much of value.

My brief sojourn at Aix re-established the ties of a growing friendship. Fauré was an extemely charming man, with a most attractive nature. He was very good to me, taking me

10

for unforgettable walks along the Lac du Bourget. The youthfullness of his character seemed to make his age vanish, and his cat-like grace, coupled with his deep-rooted inborn courtesy, belied his quiet energy through apparent nonchalance.

In retrospect I am better able to judge just how great was the privilege that allowed me to live in the wake of this great man, and that of being one of the first to be allowed to love his music. It is with some emotion that I re-read the words of Émile Vuillermoz, himself, from the first an admirer of Fauré:

> To love and understand Fauré, it is absolutely necessary to have a musical nature. Fauré is pure music, in the strictest, acoustic sense of the word. You don't have to be a musician to love Beethoven and Berlioz. But it's not the same with Fauré. If you cannot feel the physical voluptuousness of certain modulations, if you cannot taste the disturbing pungency of certain chords, if you are not interested in the subtle laws that govern the grouping of notes around a tonic, a dominant or a leading note, you will understand nothing of the disconcerting style and its apparent simplicity . . .

But, in the end, is it really necessary to analyse the why's and wherefore's of one's love to such an extent? Can't one become intoxicated with the "immortal perfume" without having to seek its source? Working on Fauré's music was one of the prides and joys of my life. If it is to favourable circumstances that I owe the privilege of having studied the piano works with the composer, no-one, I think, has played it as much as me, nor given so many pupils the feeling for the music, nor managed to pass on to so many young virtuosi this love of Fauré that they in their turn might perpetuate it.

In 1903 virtually all of Fauré's piano works had been written, with the exception of some Nocturnes and Barcarolles, the *Fantaisie* for piano and orchestra — but they remained unheard. I plunged into them, the only difficulty, among so many masterpieces, being what to choose.

I spent the rest of the summer with my sister, and, keeping to my rendez-vous, I went to Mireval to play the Franck *Quintet* with a group of amateurs formed by Comte de V . . . That fanatical Fauré enthusiast, Joseph de Marliave, decided to be presented to me this time, and even turned the pages for me. There was a young lady there in search of a husband and already she had her eye on him. When the *Quintet* was finished, he asked her, without any ill-intent, what she thought of the music. "It's nice," she replied, in a very knowing manner, and was disqualified at once.

Some time later the young officer asked me to share his life. A long engagement followed, interspersed with many happy holidays when we played music together. A very pleasant path was opening in front of us — but for how long, alas? At the side of this enlightened admirer of this music "of fantasy and reason", as he described Fauré's work, I went forward with increased confidence in the mission which I had entrusted to myself.

At the beginning of the century, our musical life was not as favourable to young players as it is today. There were no national and international competitions to reflect their glory on new names. Success was a question of being very patient. "Arriving" didn't involve that fierceness that can transform the career of the virtuoso into a merciless battle. Laurel leaves weren't heaped upon the shoulders of those just leaving adolescence. Before you could arrive, you had to leave. During this lengthy preparation you acquire a deep knowledge of your trade, and become aware of the responsibilities of the player to the work.

The rhythm of life seemed slower — but so, too, did success. What was needed was that happy combination of ability, work, enthusiasm, willingness and intelligence, too. Behind every obstacle there is hidden an element of luck. Some flounder and refuse to clear the hurdle; others meet the difficulties head-on.

I still like the motto I chose for myself: "Face things".

In a concert given in the Salle Érard in the Spring of 1903, I played, with Louis Hasslemans, the Sonata for Piano and Violin by Chevillard in the presence of the composer. Henriette Renié, the famous harpist, came to me with a message from him: "Give my greatest compliments to this young girl. Ask her to come and see me." When I was in front of Camille Chevillard, he asked me: "Would you like to play at the Concerts Lamoureux?" What a question! "But," he continued, "you know that at present they are waging war on concertos?" It was the snobbery of the day, started up under the influence of the Schola, by a few fanatics who wanted to hear of no-one other than Bach. No soloist and no concerto! "Well, do you know César Franck's *Symphonic Variations?*" "No, but I shall learn them."

I had no desire to see repeated the unexpected experience of Miss B . . . , a talented American pianist. She had been engaged by a big symphonic association, but had to abandon the idea of playing due to the violent demonstrations of an intolerant audience who had pinched the piano from the platform . . .

On Sunday, 22nd November, 1903, I made my debut at the Concerts Lamoureux in the *Symphonic Variations* of César Franck. It was a great occasion for me.[1]

Camille Chevillard was conducting. He was a typical example of the well-meaning grump, his square head and dense, crew-cut hair off-set by a huge moustache. He frightened me so much that at rehearsal I could not find the soft pedal. He used to laugh at the fright he provoked in others; and his dead-pan jokes were much feared. One of the great French conductors, he was so convincing that he told me: "I am so afraid of thunder that when I conduct the *Pastoral Symphony*, I don't feel at all at ease." He had a heart of gold, and his friendship, once given, was never withdrawn. I received so much proof of this that I shall

---

[1] It was Saint Cecilia's Day and the anniversary of my baptism. The curé of Nîmes Cathedral had been a reliable prophet when, defying my screaming, he said: "Well, this little one is bound to be a musician!"

always have the fondest memory of him.

Not long afterwards, I gave my first public performance of one of Fauré's works: it was the *Piano Quartet No. 1*. The composer turned the pages for me, and my heart was full of joy. How could anyone resist this music, full of such vitality, overflowing with life and communicative warmth, and yet so simple in its design?

As I delved further into Fauré's creative achievement, I unwittingly became his "musical possession", and he came to think that he had every claim on me. With his cigarette always at his lips, he made me study everything he loved.

During that same winter, Fauré had me learn the items of the programme for the Société Nationale, which had opened its doors to him for the first time. Among musicians this was a great occasion. The piano stood open and I had elected to play from memory, which, as far as Fauré's music was concerned, was quite novel. There were three works on the programme. I knew them well and loved them deeply: the *Third Valse-Caprice,* the *Sixth Barcarolle* and the *Fileuse* from the *Pelléas et Mélisande Suite* that Cortot had transcribed for the piano. This selection showed only one aspect of Fauré's art, but I didn't want to disappoint the expectations of the audience which had been attracted by the brilliance of the music. The flamboyance of the *Valse,* the elegance of the fine *Barcarolle* with its undulating suppleness, and the voluble *Fileuse* did, perhaps, sacrifice something to virtuosity, but was effective and nonetheless original.

It was that evening that I witnessed the astonishment of his publisher, Hamelle, in discovering the riches he had possessed for more than twenty years and which had been gathering dust on his shelves. He approached me and said: "But it's brilliant, this music of Fauré's!" His face showed his amazement and delight; he couldn't get over it. But did he know (I have this piece of information from a well-informed musician) that at one time Mme Hamelle used to cover her pots of jam with unsold works of Fauré? But this realisation did not change the policy of the Hamelle company, for in 1904 Fauré was still complaining of the neglect his music was suffering. When he was concert-going in Zürich, he declared that "not one work from Hamelle's catalogue featured in the programme, while *Shylock,* the *Pavane* and *Pélleas* ought to find a place in this orchestra, considering the nature of its concerts".[1]

Nevertheless, Fauré was delighted that evening. With characteristic modesty he attributed all the success to me. I did, at least, have the satisfaction of seeing myself accepted as the "official" interpreter of the Master by the musicians who threw themselves at me as if I were responsible for the music.

A tradition for Fauré's music had just become established. I am proud to have helped create it at the side of the composer, and to have maintained it with the unceasing work of ten years, a union of hard work and great fertility interrupted by the most unfortunate of squabbles. Until my last breath, come hell or high water, I shall continue to transmit the precious message.

[1] From a private letter.

3 The man and his image

C'est la musique souveraine qui nous fait entrevoir les vraies dimensions de l'homme. [1]

G. Duhamel

Between 1903 and 1912 my musical life was wholly in harmony with that of Gabriel Fauré. There was a bond of affection between my household and that of the composer of *La Bonne Chanson.* I was passionately fond of his music, and to serve its cause was my greatest joy.

When I got to know him better, I came to understand the duality of a character not always in harmony with the measure of his genius. I allowed also for the demands of the creative power that dwelt within him. His occasionally deceptive manner was no more than a mask for his real, deep feelings. Doubtless he caused pain, and wounded friendships offered to him in all sincerity. But was he aware of these weaknesses? Might he not have cultivated them to defend the only thing that mattered fundamentally to him: his ceaseless, fertile work?

His life as a man was conducted on the edges of his life as a musician, like two separate roads that chance occasionally brings together.

"He saw the world as a source of harmony," said Charles Koechlin, one of his most faithful pupils. It was in meditation that he discovered it. Because he had the privilege

[1] It is through sovereign music that we glimpse the true dimensions of man.

16

of a long life, he left several generations with the image of an affable but reticent man, occasionally lively, but more often taciturn.

But his knowledge of himself was very lucid, as he showed in this revealing self-portrait in answer to a letter from his wife.[1]

> You are categorical in everything. But not me. I shall die as I have lived, my mind in a state of flux.
> You have often reproached me with defending those of whom ill was spoken. I defended them because personally I didn't believe what was being said about them, because I have a basic *naïveté* (yes, na-ï-veté) which has always led me to believe good rather than evil . . . You reproach me for not speaking or for speaking very little . . .
> Allow one quality, at least, among so many faults, that of never complaining about anything. How many people would have whined when, after what they call a distinguished career, they reach old·age and its cruel infirmities (I have not heard *a single note of "Pénélope"* other than in my head) and with its poverty, because in reality, I haven't a penny to my name . . .

How can anyone read these lines without a twinge from the heart?

Gabriel Fauré's destiny was governed by certain signs with which he kept faith all his days. His true fortune lay first and foremost in being himself; the rest was of little importance. By realising the full nature of his gifts, he worked his own miracle. Nothing seemed to predestine him for music except nature's mysterious way of piling treasures on one chosen soul.

Gabriel Fauré was the sixth of a modest, cultured family, strong and close-knit. His birth had not been planned, but "we'll bring him up just like the others", his mother would have said at his birth.

That was in 1845 in the beautiful countryside of Ariège where during centuries of occupation the Saracens had settled and founded families. The super-imposed layers of

[1] From a private letter.

cultures had endowed this race with a tranquil energy and fierce independence under a tranquil exterior. Some trace of Arab blood must have run in Fauré's veins, and this unknown ancestry showed itself not just in his bronzed complexion but also in his deep, tender eyes which often seemed to catch sight of mirages. His forebears had worked with their hands. During several generations as butchers, the Faurés had acquired a solid reputation for honesty.

Gabriel's father, Toussaint Fauré, who was born in 1810, was steered towards teaching. From his first appointment as a school-teacher, he slowly climbed the official ladder. He became director of a nursery-school, sub-inspector, then inspector of primary education, and finally director of the École Normale of School-teachers in 1849.

The family circumstances at Pamiers were so precarious that the child was entrusted to a foster-mother. "He'll be a bishop, this one will," she used to say, so much did the imagination of little Gabriel astonish her. Why, hadn't he devised the service, complete with pomp and music, for the burial of . . . grasshoppers?

At the age of four he rejoined his family, and his childhood ran its smooth course in the perfumed confines of the garden at Montgauzy, which he always remembered with fondness. It was a real "priest's garden" where everything grew in abundance, with sweet-smelling flowers and fragrant plants native to that region where the mildness of the Mediterranean combines with the undulating countryside.

Opposite the hill, crowned with the medieval château of Foix, with its ramparts and towers, was Montgauzy school, which had once been a convent. It was from there that Gabriel Fauré held his earliest recollections. In the neighbouring chapel, where they still worshipped Notre Dame of Montgauzy, the chiming of the bells syncopated their rhythms with the sound of hammering from the forges in the Arget valley. The religious chants and the sound of the harmonium attracted him. Raising himself on tiptoe, he tested himself at the instrument and immersed himself in the still shapeless music. His life was free, his loneliness enchanted . . . His brothers, being older than him, were at college, his mother's time was taken up looking after the house and his father was occupied by his duties as director of the École Normale.

Several years passed in this way. Then one day fate showed its hand in the shape of an old, blind lady who heard Fauré improvise. Struck by his ability, she went to see his father and made him promise to steer the child towards a musical life by sending him to the École Niedermeyer in Paris. This school trained pupils for the duties of Maître de Chapelle. Gregorian chant, neglected by the Conservatoire, was still studied there.

Alarmed by the prospect of something so different from his natural ambitions for his son, Toussaint Fauré at first objected, arguing that the material difficulties were insurmountable; but he made inquiries just the same. Everything went smoothly. The arrival of M. Niedermeyer, during a concert tour, allowed him to hear the young musician. He decided then to take charge of his studies.

Gabriel Fauré was nine years old when he went to Paris by that picturesque route which, in 1854, brought Foix within three days of the capital. Carriages and trains, alternately, brought him towards the end of his journey. The gloomy weather of the day of his arrival chilled his child's heart.

Discipline at the École Niedermeyer was strict, comfort was unknown there, and working conditions were somewhat of a paradox — the piano was studied in groups, with fifteen instruments playing at the same time! But minds and spirits were forged there. It was there that Fauré developed the ability, later to become second nature, of withdrawing into himself. When M. Niedermeyer died in 1861, Fauré, already a very able pupil, joined Saint-Saëns's new piano class. He was fifteen and Saint-Saëns twenty-five. The two composers recalled, with considerable feeling, the years they spent at that school. Fauré always remembered it with tenderness and gratitude.

"Music was everything there," he said, and he would never stop praising the "beneficial discipline of that boarding-school which joined the teaching of the humanities with that of art and rooted in our young minds the habit of deep thought. Despite the apparent rigour of the discipline, we could, of course, be as mischievous as any schoolboy, and we got up to any number of pranks."

One of these scholars, who remained famous, showed Fauré what orchestral effects were possible, long before they were widely known. A deep and lasting friendship grew up between the composer of *Samson et Dalila* and the future composer of *Pénélope,* which Fauré was to dedicate to Saint-Saëns. This did not prevent Saint-Saëns from stating later, with his caustic wit, that Fauré was without doubt the most worthy champion of French music. He would often call him "my big fat cat", or, more tongue-in-cheek, "the unbearable animal".

His influence guided the spiritual development of his pupil whom he made familiar with the great music of Johann Sebastian Bach (who was much neglected at that time), the French harpsichord school, Mozart, Weber, Mendelssohn . . . Saint-Saëns' insatiable curiosity for everything musical led him even as far as Wagner, the most revolutionary composer of that time.

His teaching was indeed generous and without prejudice; he sought to understand everything that he might love everything. This attitude was radically different from the narrow-mindedness that still prevailed at the Conservatoire, where the pupil Massenet had just been barred from the composition class for non-conformity and independence!

Fauré still kept in touch with his family by letter and by going home in the holidays, but he was thinking of new horizons, new dreams of the future. He liked to tell of one evening, when, after seeing *Faust* at the opera, he missed the closing time of the school gate. In the company of his friend

Eugène Gigout, he spent the entire night wandering about Paris, and in the early hours of the morning they found themselves on the heights of Montmartre. There, each selected his future musical territory.

"I shall have the organ of Notre-Dame," Gigout declared.

"And I'll have the Madeleine," Fauré replied.

These were fanciful dreams which became reality.

Of all his teachers and fellow pupils, three remained true to him all his life: Saint Saëns and Gigout I have already mentioned, and André Messager, whose watchful friendship was always a source of light for him.

Now quite able to express himself in music, Fauré left the École Niedermeyer in 1865. His period of study, crowned with prizes for organ, piano and composition, was based on a solid foundation of general culture. The enchanted world of childhood was now over. Protected until then from the harsher aspects of life, Fauré now had to face its difficulties and deal with the everyday necessities which encroach on the time needed for composition. According to a Chinese proverb, "work steals much precious time".

He had already written his first song, fresh and delicate, *Le Papillon et la Fleur,* a melody with a rhythmic originality that breaks the monotony of the refrain. When, many years later, Reynaldo Hahn sent Fauré a manuscript of this early composition that he had discovered, Fauré remembered "having composed it in the school refectory among the smells from the kitchen, and having had Saint-Saëns as the first one to play it".

"It is because of this song, too," Fauré recalled, "that my name can be found in Victor Hugo's correspondence, since I needed permission before it could be published. Some meeting — insignificant and great people, small and important matters. The great poet occupied with footling author's rights!"[1]

From this period dates the *Cantique de Jean Racine,* a

[1] From a private letter of 1922.

remarkable piece whose limpid design, pure harmony and deep inspiration are wedded to the language of Racine. Fauré, it would seem, placed his abilities at the service of the most musical of our poets. The same emotional quality leads us, when we read the words of Racine, to hear the transparent music of Gabriel Fauré.

At the age of twenty Fauré was appointed organist to the Église Saint-Sauveur at Rennes. How far did his duties correspond with his own inclinations, if not with his aspirations? He was more human than mystic. He served God while developing the gifts bestowed upon him. He was attracted to the world, well received in musical salons and success greatly pleased him.

He performed scrupulously the duties assigned to him but allowed himself to be drawn, quite willingly, to the pleasures that society offered. It was to cost him his job. A punctilious priest rescinded his contract for having dared, coming from a ball at the préfecture, to appear in evening dress and white cravat at his organ bench to play at the early mass! This was an ill wind that did blow some good. On his return to Paris, Fauré was appointed to Notre-Dame de Clignancourt.

His musical activities were halted by the war of 1870. He served in the light infantry and had his baptism of fire at Champigny. After the armistice, the furies of the Commune forced him to leave Paris. When peace was declared, he was appointed to Saint Honoré d'Eylau, from where he became deputy to Charles-Marie Widor at Saint-Sulpice before taking up a post at the Madelaine in 1877. Here he succeeded Saint-Saëns as Maître de Chapelle until, replacing Théodore Dubois, he became principal organist, a position he was to hold for a good many years. And so, in addition to the work of composition that required all his energy, Fauré had to work for a living. In the winter his time was divided between giving lessons all over Paris and the demanding duties of organist.

That same year his life was brightened by a brief engagement to Marianne Viardot, the niece of Malibran, and its subsequent breaking-off wounded his heart and his pride.

The aura of the theatre, which he did not yet find particularly attractive, had blinded his future family to his gifts as a song-writer and as a composer of chamber music. When one considers that he had already written the first album of *Mélodies,* so much beautiful piano music and the *First Sonata for Piano and Violin,* one can sympathise with him at such a lack of understanding.

Overcoming his sorrow, Fauré took as his first principle to dedicate his life to music and not music to his life. His genius discovered that universe where the truths of tomorrow still lie dormant.

In 1892 his appointment as Inspector of Teaching assured him of some additional income at the cost of a considerable amount of time. His mind was kept busy and his body tired by constant journeying across France, and he fell victim to these day-to-day pre-occupations. He longed for the freedom that would allow him the leisure to work for himself. "I am occupied by so many things that there is no time left for music. That will come again . . ."[1] This quiet protest is the sad leitmotif that acts as counterpoint to his thoughts during the years when, nonetheless, he wrote his most beautiful works.

Finally, in 1897, he succeeded Massenet as Professor of Composition at the Conservatoire. The question of his nomination had already been mooted, but Ambroise Thomas, Director at the time, had vetoed it, since he held Fauré to be a dangerous revolutionary. "Fauré? Never! If he is appointed, I'll resign," he had declared indignantly.

And so Théodore Dubois had to follow the composer of *Mignon,* and Massenet, furious that his candidature had been rejected when he claimed to be appointed for life, resigned his composition class so that Fauré could take up the post. There, under his gentle discipline, many fine musicians developed their abilities, including Maurice Ravel, Florent Schmitt, Louis Aubert, Charles Koechlin, Roger Ducasse,

---

[1] In a private letter, dated 24th March, 1879.

Georges Enesco, and many others.

His well-informed, attentive teaching was characterised by artistic freedom, an attitude which was Fauré's hallmark. René Kedrick has described the class in the following colourful way: "Fauré would arrive three-quarters of an hour late, smoking his cigarette, sit down, and a few moments later he would emerge from his rêverie. 'Ravel, play your *Jeux d'eau*', he would say. Ravel would go to the piano, and after the last note had been played, the Master would make a few remarks and then return to his rêverie. After a moment he would look at his watch and nothing more would happen, the lesson being over." But it is also true, as Enesco added, with admiration and gratitude: "But we had made a lot of progress that day."

The presence of the famous teacher created a lofty and pure atmosphere, through a sort of aura that was entirely his. While others taught the tools of the trade, Fauré seemed to breathe, through his advice and his conversation, a part of his genius. There was nothing pedantic or imperious about him.

Ravel used to refer to this marvellous characteristic with emotion and admiration. He once submitted some songs to his teacher and Fauré shoved them aside. During the next class he asked to see them again. Ravel replied: "I didn't bring them; you rejected them." "Well, I could have been wrong, you know," Fauré said simply. Later, when I asked Ravel if Fauré had been fair in his assessment, and what he had done with the songs, he replied: "Fauré was right. I burned them."

In 1905 Fauré was appointed to the post of Director of the Conservatoire National de Paris. His influence breathed a new, transforming spirit into the old institution, and his reforms were so radical that they earned him the nickname of "Robespierre".

"Monsieur," Théodore Dubois told him on leaving office, "do not forget that, as its name implies, the Conservatoire is intended to conserve tradition."

But for Fauré tradition had quite a different meaning. It was rooted in his knowledge of those great classical masters on which he himself had been reared, and not in the arbitrary study of a restrictive technique. In his search for the pure source of music he rejected all conventional effects; not that he made a clean sweep of all rules and procedures, but he wished to apply them anew in the clearness of "un langage transmissible entre un et quelques-uns" (Mallarmé).[1] "To know an art really well," Fauré would say, "one must know everything about it, both its origins and its development."

He put his dilemma in these words: "How many times have I asked myself what use music is? And what am I translating? What feelings? What ideas? How can I express something I do not understand myself?"[2] Here one can understand, from life itself, the drama of creation and the misgivings which assail the creator in search of himself. One can understand that he should refuse to codify music, since he trusted only in the natural evolution of his perception.

From 1905 official honours were showered upon Fauré who remained so modest, apparently without ambition. In 1909 he entered the Institut, not without meeting yet once more an obstinate wall of "conservatives". He himself saw in his success only devotion to the progressive work he was carrying out as Directeur of the Conservatoire, which drew this comment from a foreign colleague, who was professor at Geneva: "The thrust that M. Fauré has given Paris will have the effect of an earthquake and will wake from their torpor all the conservatories of Europe."[3]

He then abandoned his duties of inspector of music and left his post as music critic to *Le Figaro* through whose columns his opinion carried much weight. Only the pursuit of composing and the slow development of his career were of any importance.

[1] "a language that can pass between one and many"
[2] From a private letter.
[3] From a private letter.

Time seemed to have no hold on him. Gabriel Fauré lost nothing of the freshness of his ideas or his delicate sensitivity. Under his silver hair, he was as bold and supple as an adolescent, remaining straightforward and unassuming. One day, when he was due to go to meet a minister, he asked Paul Léon, Director of the Beaux-Arts, to accompany him. To the latter's astonishment, Fauré said to him: "Well, you see, it always overwhelms me a bit . . . My father was just an instituteur." This is supreme modesty from a man really far above others.

Nonetheless, it did require a great amount of personal effort for Fauré to conceal his torment. For some years already, a terrible ailment, the worst that could possible affect a musician, had been making his life more and more painful . . . Gabriel Fauré felt and knew that he was going deaf: "I am shattered by this illness which affects me in that very thing that it would have been vital for me to keep intact. It is disrespectful or, at the very least, hardly thoughtful to recall Beethoven." Nevertheless, the second part of his life was filled with despair: "Now, there are some periods of music, some pitches of which I can hear nothing . . . of my music as well as of others. I feel that there is on my shoulders nothing more than a terrible cloak of misery and discouragement."[1]

When one considers the innumerable works created in the cruel conditions of the isolation where his illness threw him, one is astounded. Fernand Bourgeat, who accompanied Fauré when he visited the house in Bonn where Beethoven was born, told me of the fierce emotion that gripped Fauré in front of the hearing devices that tortured Beethoven. What comparisons must he have made then?

In spite of the torment caused by his hearing, his head was full of music and his inspiration seemed unaffected by his worries. He was the creator of a world of sound whose elements he drew from within his own being, and his work,

---

[1] From a letter dated August, 1903, when he composed the *Andante* of the *Quintet in E minor*.

affected by the inroads of age, became more spiritual. His greatest regret was that he did not have enough time to compose, he met with obstacle after obstacle, his every composition was the product of lengthy deliberation, work required an immense effort from him ("It is like a sticking door that I have to open," he told us), and yet this was the man who left us a body of work whose importance and quality make it one of the summits of human thought. He denied the presence of inspiration: "Without work, which is art, it is nothing," he said. "Say only that which is of value, or stay silent" was the credo of his entire existence. Maurice Ravel would often quote the words of Jean Racine's son: "My father has always had difficulty in turning an easy verse".

His *String Quartet* carries the opus number 121, and in this number many pages of religious music, and above all *Pénélope,* are not included.

In 1920 Gabriel Fauré resigned himself, not without regret, to leaving the directorship of the Conservatoire. He had, alas, become almost completely deaf, and his health was in the balance.

As compensation for this loss of position he received the badge of *Grand Officier de la Légion d'Honneur.* Congratulations poured in from all sides to this man who recognised only the ephemeral character of honours. Nature, which he loved and admired, offered him greater consolation than mankind. But he was moved by so many "true letters, touching demonstrations from people I had forgotten, or by whom I might have thought myself forgotten . . ."

His quiet irony did not weaken. Philippe Erlanger has told me that when Gabriel Fauré announced his appointment to Robert Brussel, then *Directeur de l'Action Artistique,* he added: "What would give me pleasure is to have cannons fired at my funeral!

The friendly vigilance of Paul Léon, the Director of the Beaux-Arts, was a source of further comfort to him. The termination of his pension had once more brought into question the precarious nature of his means of existence. He preferred to any empty promises that he be paid the pension that was due to him. Eventually Fauré acquired the liberty to which he had aspired all his life. He could travel as he wished and work without constraint.

It was as if he was devoured by the need to create. During this first winter he wrote, almost without effort, the *Second Piano Quintet* and the three songs of *L'Horizon Chimérique*, to poems of the young poet Jean de la Ville de Mirmont, who was killed on the field of honour. But he was becoming tired more quickly. "Everything always arrives too late." Periods of immeasurable weariness when he could not work would be followed by days of happiness when he would be visited by inspiration.

To put aside one last time the poverty that threatened Fauré because of the increased cost of living, one of his most faithful friends, M. M . . . , with the generous help of many others, organised a festival of Fauré's music at the Sorbonne. It was a demonstration of national homage which was offered fervently to him, in that unforgettable evening of 1922, and of which he could distinguish only a confused noise.

He had now only a few years to live, and his physical forces were on the decline, but he enriched his œuvre with some sublime pages which reached those elevated spheres where the soul communicates in immortality. Right up to the end, he remained lucid, and humble before his music.

Finally, on his last evening, he said: "When I am no more, you will hear said of my work: 'After all, it is only so much . . .'. You will detach yourself from it, perhaps . . . All that has no importance. I have done what I could . . . and so, judge, my God." Those were his last words.

With the death of Gabriel Fauré, one of the greatest musicians of all time passed away. But when approaches were made to the government for a state funeral, the minister whose authorisation was required went so far as to ask: "But who was this Gabriel Fauré?" It required the intervention of Paul Léon and Louis Barthou to enlighten him.

At the Madeleine, where for so long Fauré had made the great organ sing, the ceremony proceeded in magnificence, underlining with its pomp the contrast with the simplicity of a life whose genius alone reached greatness.

4 *The piano works of Gabriel Fauré*

Among Gabriel Fauré's compositions there are some to which, more than to others, I remain devotedly attached. One such is the *Ballade* for piano and orchestra, with which I made my debuts at the Société des Concerts du Conservatoire. To play there meant acceptance, and this I owe to the *Ballade*.

The duties of Director of the Conservatoire include those of Honorary President of the Société, and it is thanks to Gabriel Fauré that I played there for the first time in 1907.

Founded by Habeneck in 1826 to make Beethoven's symphonies known in France, the prestige of the Société is still as great, but at the beginning of the century access to it was, so to speak, closed to the young. Only the greatest artists could be heard there: Liszt, Sarasate, Planté, Paderewski, Busoni, and many other celebrities wrote their names in the Golden Book. My emotion was great when I came to write my name beside those of the famous to perpetuate the memory of my debuts and the long association which followed them. I have been an honorary member of the Société since 1937.

At that time there was only a small number of concerts given annually. Even Frédéric Chopin had been turned down. I have seen with my own eyes his letter of application, written in his delicate, aristocratic hand and dated 13th March, 1832. He was then twenty-two. Addressed to *Messieurs les membres du Comité de la Société des Concerts*, it reads:

Messieurs, I should like to be granted the favour of performing at one of your admirable concerts, and this I beg to ask of you. Trusting, since I lack other qualifications to obtain this, in your goodwill towards artists, I dare to hope that you will greet my request favourably, I have the honour to be, Messieurs, your very humble servant.

Frédéric Chopin
Cité Bergère, No. 4

Paris, 13th March, 1832.

In the margin of the original one can read the laconic and brutal reply: *Request received too late.* And yet, Robert Schumann, when he heard some of Chopin's earliest works, had already saluted him in one of his articles with his famous "Hats off, gentlemen, a genius!"

"Make room for the young" was not a fashionable slogan in those days. A distrustful public demanded much proof. To manage to get oneself heard often required a chain of favourable circumstances, as well as the necessary talent. One cannot imagine today what an engagement from the famous Société meant to a young artist. The conditions were purely honorary, but the silver medal one received had a value beyond price. It is true that it was accompanied by the sum of "100 Francs for gloves and carriages". Carriages one can still understand, but one wonders just what a "glove allowance" might mean to a pianist! Nevertheless Saint-Saëns used to come on to the platform with his hands gloved. At the moment he was to begin playing he would put his gloves down on the desk and start his programme.

The concerts had always taken place in the old Salle des Concerts at the Conservatoire which enjoyed the reputation of having perfect acoustics. André Messager thought that this was a rather exaggerated judgement, saying of the hall: "It is cruel".

The audience was a world on its own, a sort of musical aristocracy which liked to consider itself part of this elevated class, and it was regarded as one of the high points of musical life.

The seats, except for those in the amphitheatre, were sold

entirely by subscription. The size of the audiences meant that that two concert series, A and B, were required; the programmes were repeated on alternate Sundays. There were always fierce struggles at the box-office over the few empty seats.

The subscriptions were treated like family heirlooms, and were handed down in wills, even making a much appreciated wedding-present. It was quite the thing to be seen at the Conservatoire concerts, and with this privilege went the right to certain opinions; indeed, reputations were established there. The tastes cultivated here were conservative; a certain hostility reigned, as much towards new works as new artists, and especially towards women. Thus I had a triple obstacle to overcome: my youth, the fact that I was a woman, and the championship of an almost unknown work.

It was my good fortune that Gabriel Fauré, whose *Ballade* I was playing, wanted it to be heard at the Société des Concerts. It could not be considered a novel work, but in 1907 it still had not been featured on the programmes of any major concerts. It was a great honour for me to be giving the work its first performance in front of an audience reputed to be the most difficult in the capital.

Fauré had composed his *Ballade* in 1881 in an original version for solo piano, his first work for piano after the composition of so many songs; it confirmed the unshakeably French temperament and genius of its creator.

In the years 1877 to 1879 Fauré still had not escaped from the Wagnerian influences he had come under on his visits to Bayreuth with his friend Camille Saint-Saëns. But however overwhelmed he may have been, his music still retained its individuality. His inspiration, devoid of grandiose gestures, showed itself through charm, modesty, restraint, and freshness of expression. The sublety of his modulations and lively but unaffected accentuations are characteristic of his type of genius. The spirit of Verlaine informed his tastes, his instincts.

But sometimes he had misgivings about the boldness of his

own accents, and trusting the opinion of his peers, he would willingly seek their criticism.

From 1877 Saint-Saëns, always his friend and often his guide, had taken him to Weimar where, at the instigation of Liszt, the Grand Duke had seen to the staging of the première of *Samson et Dalila* which the Opéra de Paris had refused. One can imagine the emotion that Fauré must have felt at this meeting with the legendary Franz Liszt.

When in 1882, Fauré met Liszt again in Zürich, he submitted to him the manuscript of the *Ballade* which he had just written. "I was rather afraid that it might be too long," Fauré told me, "and I said this to Liszt, who gave me the marvellous reply: 'Too long, young man, has no meaning. One writes as one thinks.' " The composer of *Mazeppa* was certainly not the man to be surprised by lengthy developments.

The novelty of Fauré's writing disconcerted Liszt. Although he acknowledged the interest of the work, he sent it back to him, as he found it too difficult. Obviously Liszt was very old, and this very original piano technique had surprised and, no doubt, unsettled him.

It is the forfeit of old age to remain rooted sometimes in one's own epoch. I remember the confession of my old friend, Francis Planté, who, although he retained an interest in all things new, had not been able to come to terms with the evolution of a novel technique in a very difficult Étude which Roger Ducasse had dedicated to him: "I am afraid there are some works on which I shall have to draw the curtain," he confessed to me. And so the flame of progress marches ever on . . .

In the orchestral version of the *Ballade*, the piano writing is "now and then one stage removed from the harmonic activity in the orchestra", but the traps for the memory are still there. Before studying Fauré's music I had never feared a loss of memory and only then did I begin to mistrust my memory, a fear which has never really left me. But the only thing that matters is how one plays the music.

Let us return to the day of the twin debuts of the *Ballade* and myself at the Société des Concerts du Conservatoire. When this important Sunday arrived I felt strengthened by my long preparation under the guidance of the composer and Georges Marty, the famous conductor.

My emotion was all the greater for knowing just how much this performance meant for Fauré, too. I can remember walking through the narrow door that led to the wings of the concert hall and the seemingly interminable wait before going onto the platform.

While the piano was being moved into place, I was overcome with fright. To calm me down, Fauré complimented me on the lovely dress I was wearing. It was of white muslin with gold flowers. "Oh," he cried, "what a very pretty dress in F sharp major, quite in the key of the *Ballade*!"

"Yes, perhaps, but that doesn't stop me not knowing how it begins."

"Then I wouldn't worry: it's not you that begins, it's the orchestra!"

An observation all the more amusing for the fact that, the orchestra does begin the piece, it only plays one note, an F sharp which serves as a base for the solo piano's opening chords.

The work was relatively successful. It made me very annoyed that the praise was directed at me rather than at the *Ballade*: "Your playing is so very lovely, Madame, but what obscure music".

Gabriel Fauré, in his modesty, was satisfied with his interpreters. He simply said to Georges Marty and to me, with that lovely smile that would light up his face: "That is something realised for me".

The work, with its fresh and novel poetry, was too far in advance of its time.

One attentive observer, however, had noticed an encouraging sign. There was in the audience an old subscriber who disliked all contemporary music. To show his

disapproval he would make great play of reading his news-
paper, *Le Temps,* held wide open, while the offending work
was being performed. On this day he was seen to raise an
inquisitive eye during the playing of the *Ballade* and abandon
his reading for a few moments, thus showing his interest in
this delightful music.

Happily, the time of incomprehension is over, and the
clarity of the *Ballade* has since been accorded its fair share of
glory, although it has been burdened with a good number of
inaccurate assessments. Some critics relate it to the spirit of
Debussy, forgetting that the *Ballade* is several years older
than it. Fauré's approach to the *Ballade* is, indeed, entirely
original, although it does revive a specifically Romantic
genre.

> "Fauré, the direct heir of Chopin, has carried through all
> the methods of composition that one finds in the work of the
> Polish genius and in that of Liszt. He transforms them into his
> own style and goes further down the path opened by Chopin,
> since he feels all the expressive value of pure harmony. Chopin,
> Fauré — two of the piano's greatest lyricists."

In Fauré's *Ballade* everything is pure music; there is no
oratory, no echo of passionate feelings, but a limpid, harmonious joy in the creation of music. Fauré weaves with
sound according to the wishes of his imagination.

What work fits better than the *Ballade* this luminous
description that Joseph de Marliave wrote in 1909 in his
Études Musicales?

> On the one hand, you have what appears to be a dazzling
> capriccio, overflowing with spirit, with the unexpected, with
> verve, and on the other hand, there is a lucid and sturdy logic
> that informs the piece with a firm will, served by the most
> precise skill, by the most brilliant technique.

If I have had the pride of contributing to its success by
playing the *Ballade* as often as possible in front of the
most varied audiences, I have reaped much joy from it,
as well as innumerable memories. Some are quite funny,

as at Marseilles where my performance of the *Ballade* was its first in that town. I was visited in the foyer by two ladies who seemed very interested in the lively discussion they were having before they came up to me. When they reached me, one of them said: "Mademoiselle, allow me to touch your dress — my friend and I would like to know what it is made of..." Then off they went without saying another word.

Our art is both glory and service. You work, you fight... and then some-one deals you a back-handed compliment like that. But it is a salutary shock and a good lesson in humility, nonetheless.

My recollection of the 1949 Edinburgh Festival is much more comforting. There I played the *Ballade* under the baton of Roger Désormières, along with the Ravel *Concerto in G,* both of which were encored as usual. I remember with joy the lines which appeared in an important London weekly: "The memory of the Festival will long have disappeared when that of Marguerite Long's playing of Fauré's *Ballade* is still remembered by all those who heard it".

In 1954 the Société des Concerts du Conservatoire asked me to play the *Ballade* under André Cluytens to commemorate the thirtieth anniversary of Fauré's death. The Théâtre des Champs-Elysées was packed, I was recalled again and again, and the audience was shouting enthusiastically for the *Ballade* to be encored. Knowing that I was not well, André Cluytens said to me: "Don't tire yourself out".

"What? Forty-seven years ago, in this very society, I was told that the *Ballade* was obscure, today they're shouting for an encore and you think I'm not going to play it again?" And it went down even better the second time round.

Is Gabriel Fauré's music not understood abroad, and is his language a sealed book beyond the borders of France? The same thing was said of Brahms whose music is now so highly regarded in France simply because courageous musicians, convinced of its beauty, went out of their way to get it heard.

The desire for effect too often influences the preparation

of programmes. Of course, an artist knows he will be be more successful if he plays familiar works, while it requires a great deal of faith to champion modern music which is still unknown to the general public. But the rewards are considerable when the effort bears fruit!

Fauré's music would have the audience abroad its beauty deserves, if it were played there more often. As long as this music was limited by such tags as "intimate music", "charming" or "half-coloured", these marvellous riches remained the prerogative of refined coteries.

My own experience proves that in the most varied of countries Fauré's music can arouse the same enthusiasm. Recently, in 1954, I played the *Ballade* for the fiirst time on my tour of South America, and the reception was so favourable that I decided to put it back in one of my Jeunesses Musicales programmes.

The municipal theatre was packed, there were people sitting on the platform, the national anthems were played, and, that night too, the *Ballade* was encored. The heat was stifling, but I would not swear that the tears I wiped away from my eyes with my handkerchief were caused by the heat alone.

The rehearsal had been excellent. It had finished very late and I was getting ready to leave when one of the orchestral musicians rose and went over to speak quietly to the conductor. My good friend Eléazar de Carvalho then said to me: "The orchestra wonders if it would not be too much to ask you to play the *Ballade* again. This time they want to hear it played for them." Isn't it wonderful that orchestral musicians should ask such a thing?

During my first tour of the USSR in 1955, I had the honour of renewing the cultural links between our two countries, thus opening the way to artistic exchange. The tour was to begin with a concert in Moscow.

The Franco-Soviet programme included, among other things, Ravel's *Concerto in G* and Fauré's *Ballade*. Unfortuneately, an attack of flu had forced me to postpone the concert for a few days. To conserve my strength, only the Ravel *Concerto* had been kept in the programme, which also included Shostakovich's *Symphony No. 1* and Ravel's *La Valse*.

After I had played the concerto, the applause was considerable and, as usual, I had to repeat the finale. The insatiable audience was clapping to the beat of the now familiar rhythm. Then some of the orchestral players started begging me: "Oh, madame, Fauré, Fauré . . ." How could I resist? With no other rehearsal than a simple run-through several days beforehand, the orchestra, under the baton of that eminent Soviet conductor, Kyril Kondrashin, led the *Ballade* to victory. Perhaps never again will the now-famous *Ballade* be played with more fervour. It gave me much joy to be able to bring the orchestra, and especially the remarkable flautist, into that triumph. Of all my memories, those I have just recalled in connection with the *Ballade* remain my most precious.

When I read a young critic, in an article on Fauré, saying that "no-one has stood up for Fauré", I was outraged. We would be most to blame if we let such idiocies come to be believed. One would have to be ill-informed (or ill-intentioned) to dare to voice such an opinion when Fauré's music can be heard all round the world.

I much prefer Maurice Ravel's spontaneous admission: on one of the grand tours I undertook with him in 1932, in Europe and in America, to perform his *Concerto in G,* which was written for me, and which was often accompanied on the programme by the *Ballade,* Ravel said to me, after a rehearsal: "Ah, it's lovely, the *Ballade,* it really is delightful. I am unfair to Fauré's music in so far as I don't know it very well. When we get back, you'll have to play me lots of it." I know nothing more touching than this bit of retrospective homage paid to Gabriel Fauré by his greatest pupil.

5 *The story of an appointment*

Life, so sparing with its gifts, brought me unalloyed happiness in the year 1906. I was married to Joseph de Marliave, with Fauré and Marmontel as witnesses; I received my first appointment as Professor at the Conservatoire; and I worked unflaggingly with the composer of *Prométhée*. An admirer of Fauré from the first, my husband could play the piano accompaniments of the songs from memory and was acquainted with every detail of the piano music.

I was still on my honeymoon when a telegram arrived from my teacher, Antonin Marmontel, telling me that a preparatory class at the Conservatoire had just fallen vacant and urging me to apply. At that time piano classes were in two stages, each given to a different teacher: preparatory (keyboard), and superior.

Gabriel Fauré, nevertheless, did not immediately subscribe to the idea of my appointment, saying it would be better to wait until a superior class became vacant. Under the influence of Marmontel, he changed his mind, having an inkling that my presence would bring a real atmosphere of youthfulness to that great school.

I was much attracted by the idea of being a professor at the Conservatoire, and, without encountering any more obstacles, I was appointed. I began my "apostleship" with enthusiasm. Gone were the days when I would look up at the clock whose hands didn't seem to move during lessons, whether at the lesson of the unbearable urchin who had continually to be grabbed by his sailor's collar to keep him

39

at the piano, or of the old lady who wouldn't let me off for a moment. 1907 saw the beginning of that series of competitions where so many pupils made me proud. I can still see Fauré arriving at my house to announce the success of my class from that first year and saying: "There is some-one even happier than you are, and that's Marmontel". He was on the jury.

Three weeks later Marmontel died suddenly in the street, at a time when his liveliness, for a professor of a superior class, was still astonishing those around him. I lost a great friend; and the years have not erased my grateful memory. I would have liked to take over his class at the Conservatoire to transmit his marvellous knowledge of the piano which, thanks to his care, I had in my blood. The Director, however, had other ideas.

To adorn the Conservatoire with new lustre, Fauré called upon the services of the artists who were most representative of that time. He had already had the following appointed: Paul Dukas, Vincent d'Indy, Édouard Risler, the great violinist, Lucien Capet, Camille Chevillard. He wrote me a long and beautiful letter promising me the next class which would then, he said, "be mine by right". His promise was formal: "You will find me resolute and steadfast in favour of your appointment".

I resigned myself to it all the more easily because I found the work of my young pupils interesting. I was serving an apprenticeship here which would help me throughout my teaching career. To that which I had learned from my teachers I added my own observations, and my experience broadened. The truth of the matter is that if no-one, of all the millions on this planet, has the same face, no-one has the same hands, or the same abilities — this is what makes teaching so exciting, but difficult. The "do as I do" of some teachers is nonsense.

I did not mind having to prolong this stage, and was given strength by the promise that its duration would be limited . . . But it was to take me fourteen years to reach a superior class.

It cost me some fighting and a good deal of disillusionment. It is not without bitterness that I recall here the troubled time which followed.

A muffled struggle began to develop slowly. I refused to attribute to Gabriel Fauré's own will an attitude which was certainly dictated to him and which I later knew to have caused him pain. The consequences, which were to change the teaching structure at the Conservatoire so profoundly through the creation of mixed piano classes, instead of the old formula of separate classes for boys and girls, could not then have been predicted.

But let us not get ahead of ourselves. If all this sad story was to reveal to me the nastiness of certain emotions, this did not come about until the time when a superior class was about to become vacant.

In the years 1906 to 1912, not a shadow came to darken our relationship with Gabriel Fauré. It was during this period that I saw Fauré almost daily, working at his music with him, playing it everywhere and doing everything I could to make it better known. By playing it in many countries where it was still unknown — and uplifting myself with it — I have been able, consequently, to detach myself from all the complications of those goings-on and to remain true to my real mission of being an interpreter of Fauré's music.

In 1913, that remarkable teacher, dear, great Delaborde, died. Immediately some of the people round Fauré did their best to prevent him keeping his promise. The fear that I might be granted this class transformed into a furious mob those who, up till now, had been content just to let me live. They played the role of evil counsellors, leading Gabriel Fauré to commit an illegal act.

The regulation which governs the administration of the Conservatoire is that the Upper Council alone is entitled to appoint professors — without exception. Now, M. Fauré, on his authority alone, had transferred M. Victor Staub from a class of men to a class of women. However skilful this bit of juggling might have appeared, it was none the less distressing.

Had I been single, I do not know what I would have done, but fortunately my husband was at my side and his reaction reflected his indignation. He understood the dangers that this manoeuvre would create in the future. He had me apply for the men's class, the only one vacant since Staub had been "slipped along". Although he knew that my appointment to this class was impossible, he wanted to underline with this gesture the abuse of power.

The Upper Council was alerted; one of its members took it upon himself to answer the questions which were bound to be raised, and stressed the reasons that had led me to take up this position, the only one possible to validate what I considered a right acquired with that formal, written, promise made now already seven years ago.

The campaign that was getting under way threatened to become lively. To stifle its inevitable repercussions, two great musicians asked me to withdraw my candidacy and promised me a myriad different compensations — but it paid me not to take them at face value. My husband had no illusions: the future could not have held better prospects if the rules had not been changed.

According to the inescapable law of age, the next class was to be made vacant by the most elderly professor. This was the aged Louis Diémer, himself the teacher of a class of boys. In order to avoid a repetition of the same difficulties, a solution had to be found. It was then that my husband hit upon the ingenious idea of mixed piano classes, such as already existed for the violin, where boys and girls worked together. Once this reform had been allowed, argument number one against me was automatically invalid. There would no longer be any obstacle to professors of either sex teaching equally in all the classes. He then countered all other arguments against me before taking his next steps, and once he had started, nothing stopped him. He had a word with some of his député friends, alerted the chairman of the Budget Commission, and undertook a veritable campaign in favour of establishing mixed piano classes. He was convinced that everyone would gain from joint teaching, bringing together the girls, often better workers, with the boys, who were often better musicians. Emulation would bring better results.

The detailed report for which he was asked was so convincing that it was reproduced just as it stood and inserted in the general report of the Beaux-Arts, and then was adopted by the Commission. These are the facts as they happened, establishing mixed piano classes at the Conservatoire. This reform was, at the beginning of the century, one of the most successful.

Between Gabriel Fauré and me, things were beginning to become acrimonious. Fauré was called to the Ministry in a spirit of conciliation. I received all the necessary overtures of peace: a favourable solution had to be found.

But this was 1914. The great drama was about to burst on the world, crushing man, things and ideas. No-one was spared. This terrible ordeal was to cost me my happiness. In August, 1914, my life's union, so close, so perfect, was about to be shattered. Events occurred with frenzied speed. The catastrophe swept down on me, taking me completely unprepared, thrown off balance in this tragic whirlwind.

On 2nd August, general mobilisation assembled all the able-bodied men in the country; on 12th August my husband, Captain Joseph de Marliave, left to join his unit; on 24th August a bullet in the heart, I was told, put an end to such a noble life. He was only just forty years old.

Then came the horrible waiting, the tragic lack of news, the glimmers of hope, then suddenly, the certain knowledge, thick as a winding-sheet, that everything was over. I had to wait five years to tend that corner of the earth where I was told he had fallen. Among so many of the nameless dead, lying side by side, the open tomb has kept its secret for ever.

He had no other epitaph than Capitaine inconnu.

I enveloped myself in silence, my grief shutting me off from the world. Days passed without my being able to accept the sacrifice. Renunciation seemed my only refuge. Music alone was a source of comfort. It was that which saved me.

In April, 1917, after three years of this life, devoid of any activity, my dear friends Camille Chevillard and Gabriel Pierné urged me to play in public again. During the war the Colonne and Lamoureux concert associations had been amalgamated. Their two conductors persuaded me to agree to play at a concert they were giving for the benefit of their prisoners. How could anyone refuse such a request? With an effort I stifled my grief and agreed to co-operate. It was with Vincent d'Indy's *Symphonie Cévenole,* under the baton of Camille Chevillard, that I made my return. The concert took place at the Salle Gaveau.

Upon my arrival in the wings I could hear the heart-gripping sounds of the Marseillaise, played to an audience standing in excited awe. For me this moment was both sublime and terrible. I steeled my will and my courage carried me through.

I shall always remember with grateful affection these two great musician friends, who, by their brotherly gesture, restored me to my art.

During that same year, 1917, I rejoined Claude Debussy at Saint-Jean-de-Luz and resumed the work I had begun with him in 1914. [1] Musical life regained a little of its activity, and a new current drew me on. The Société Musicale Indépendante re-opened. It gathered together "progressive" musicians under the presidency of Gabriel Fauré, its founder, who, since he had not been able to merge the old Société Nationale with the S.M.I., retained his connection with both groups.

One student dear to Fauré was Roger Ducasse, a friend of long standing, who had brought me his *Études* for piano. I opened the inaugural session of the S.M.I. by giving the first performances of two of these very difficult pieces.

[1] *At the Piano with Debussy,* Marguerite Long (J. M. Dent & Sons, London, 1972)

As soon as the Société Nationale re-opened, I gave there the first performances of some of Claude Debussy's admirable *Études,* written in 1915 and a real synthesis of his œuvre. Some time later, Maurice Ravel brought me his *Tombeau de Couperin,* an astonishing memorial.

My career as a virtuoso had restarted and I was still occupied in teaching. The question of my appointment at the Conservatoire, which had been lying dormant during the war, was re-opened at the end of 1919 with the death of Louis Diémer, a great teacher and a great friend. With it, battle was recommenced. For the pupils of Maître Diémer, the way seemed clear for one of them to succeed him. The idea of a woman being selected did not even occur to them. Nevertheless, Louis Diémer himself had given me proof of his regard for me by sending me this message when one of his pupils was giving an audition: "Dear Madame, I would be very pleased to see you on Tuesday at the Salle Érard, to hear, and give me your treasured advice on my pupils. With great affection, Louis Diémer."

My husband's predictions were about to come true, but now I was to fight and overcome alone the obstacles that would be raised before me. In reality, nothing should have opposed my appointment. My candidacy was justified not only by the formal promises that had been made again and again, but by my increasing reputation as a pedagogue. Alas, I came up against the fierce hostility of Gabriel Fauré. It had still the same source, the same grounds. He could not deny what he had written in his letter but looked for every possible excuse.

He collected unimaginable arguments in favour of a candidate he hoped would oppose me. It was argued that teaching at superior level had never been entrusted to a woman, forgetting the precedents of Mme. Massart and Mme. Farenc, lost, it is true, in the mists of time. All the world seemed allied against me. On one side, the men did not like female competition in what they regarded as their territory, and, on the other, the women, seeing in me nothing more than a rival, forgot that in reality I was clearing the path for them. I had to wage a veritable academic campaign.

I have an amusing memory of certain visits to some members of the Upper Council who showed themselves to be unbelievably stupid and lacking in understanding. Nothing was spared me. One of them even went so far as to say that "since a woman's hand is different from a man's, I couldn't expect to teach boys"! There were all sorts of nonsensical reasons invented to thwart my appointment.

Although it was so many years ago, I can still see myself with one of those gentlemen, and a real musician to boot, who tried to move me to pity bewailing his own fate. "Believe me, Madame," he said to me, "all the world has its share of bitterness. I am fifty-six years old, and never have had any performances." I sympathised readily with the injustice of his lot without letting it interfere with my purpose.

So much trouble was taken under the false pretext that the three boys left from Diémer's class could not study under the direction of a woman! Never was my treasured motto, "Face things", needed more than then.

I discovered a wealth of energy in myself. Fortunately, I was sustained by brotherly friendships. And then I felt myself borne up by an inner force which I associated with the spirit of my husband. What he had wanted was about to come about. Since I hated asking the slightest thing for myself, I defended my career vehemently. And then, as always, the young were with me. Darius Milhaud, whom I did not yet know, bore witness of this to me: "We are all with you", he told me.

On the morning of the day when the Upper Council was to meet to deliberate on the famous election, I was taking the collection for the benefit of prisoners of war from the Conservatoire during a service that had taken place in the Protestant church of the Étoile. At my nerve's end, I could not bear the sight of the flags, the speeches telling of human misery, the sound of the national anthems, the blare of the trumpets. I burst into tears . . . it was more than I could cope with.

In spite of the open betting, my trials were nearly over. At last, by dint of battling on, I won my appointment. There was one funny thing: as she left the Upper Council, Rose Caron said loudly: "What, Marguerite Long has been appointed? I thought they didn't want any women . . ." And she was on the jury!

The next day M. Paul Léon, then Director General of the Beaux-Arts, gave me my finest reward. When I went to see him, on an official visit, he greeted me with these unforgettable words: "I am happy, Madame, because it is rare to be able to combine matters of friendship and the general interest".

In the flood of congratulations that swept over me, it was not difficult to distinguish the sincere feelings of my friends from the bitter-sweet words of those who had fought me to the last. Then came the procession of photographers, journalists, flowers; in a word, the usual ballyhoo that accompanies success. I was satisfied that the cause of women had triumphed.

I remained alert, careful to fulfil worthily the important functions entrusted to me, knowing, through the example of my predecessors, that nothing great can be achieved if one does not respect the rules. Exactitude and precision were the watchwords of my life, so that it could never be said: "That's what you get if you appoint a woman". The achievements of this "woman's class" were brilliant enough for me to present them without false modesty.

From 1920 to 1940, during the twenty years that I was teaching a superior class, I tood pride in training some of the best pupils of the Conservatoire and in proving that boys, as well as girls, have brought me honour. The names that I could write are just too many to be able to quote here. Just as people used to speak of the pupils of Louis Diémer, I wished that in the same way one might refer to someone as a pupil of Marguerite Long. I had at heart the continuation of a great pianistic tradition, the transmission to my pupils of my deep knowledge of the works of the great geniuses I have been privileged to know and who chose me to play their music: Gabriel Fauré, Claude Debussy and Maurice Ravel.

6 My first recital of Fauré in 1909

There are some actions whose boldness time alone removes. To give a recital of Gabriel Fauré's piano works in 1909 was a daring move. The public, hardly used to the subtleties of the style, was unmoved — the worst form of indifference. It would be better to stir up violent feelings. For a long time Gabriel Fauré remained an unknown genius.

I still remember the painful ordeal he underwent in 1907, on the evening that the Société Nationale had programmed the première of Maurice Ravel's *Histoires Naturelles* in a concert that ended with Fauré's *Piano Quartet No. 1,* with the composer at the keyboard. The audience's interest was centred on the Ravel work which the recent scandal of the withholding of the Prix de Rome had made famous. Yet, again, snobbishness unleashed passions.

The work, zealously advocated by Jane Bathori, had aroused a storm of protests. Jules Renard's text was answered in the hall by stupid onomatopoeic noises. It was one of those examples of the idiocy of humans when faced with a masterpiece. There was, however, a small number of ardent defenders who reacted violently against those who said the *Histoires Naturelles* were incomprehensible.

This Hernani-style battle[1] finished, leaving the hall half-empty. Only the real friends were left to hear the *Quartet*. Fauré's bitterness was all the keener for the fact that Maurice

---

[1] When Victor Hugo's play *Hernani* was first produced, there was a riot in the theatre.

Ravel had been his pupil.

It would hardly have been astonishing, then, to discover at the back of Fauré's character the dreaded shadow of jealousy. This sentiment, as circumstance decreed, was one of the components of his character. He was reproached for it, just as he was for self-seeking. Poor, dear, great Fauré — what irony and what injustice to find oneself accused of behaviour that is imposed by fate. If his life had not been so difficult, worries about money spared him, and if the critics had shown themselves understanding of his work, jealousy would have had no hold on him.

Fauré's stature was recognised only very late, and the innovative quality of his music was not understood in his own time. Later, in fact, almost too late, the revelations afforded by the music of Claude Debussy and Maurice Ravel had changed the course of musical history . . . but just a little chronology would have sufficed to put everything in its rightful place.

By setting against him, as if rivals, those whose forerunner he was, and one of whom he had even taught, what feelings could one expect to see awakened in him? A heavy responsibility to posterity is carried by those who, for so long, saw in Fauré a "salon musician", a pejorative epithet when applied to his work, which is so powerful in its concentrated expression and so well constructed despite its appearance of charm and sensitivity. For a long time I had been aware of the strength of its message and was getting ready to advocate its truth.

It was during the holidays that, under the guidance of the composer, I deepened my knowledge of his works. I remember the summer of 1907 when my husband and I went to join him at Lugano. Fauré was then working on the composition of *Pénélope* and Marliave helped him to recopy the music he had already written.

Sometimes inspiration would escape him, and while he struggled with the composition of a difficult scene, he would drag me off on endless walks, hardly speaking, walking with his hands behind his back, with a rapid step that I could hardly keep up with. In the evening we would play *belote*, but if I won, he would not speak to me the next day! Twice a week, on Thursdays and Sundays, the evenings were devoted to music.

Some distance from Lugano, in the castle at Trevano, there lived a rather curious person. M. Lombard, a former violinist, had acquired a considerable fortune in America from extra-musical speculation. As the owner of this castle which boasted a theatre, he had hired, to occupy his hours of leisure during the summer, the orchestra of La Scala, Milan . . . which he liked to conduct.

In the evening, his guests had the enjoyable privilege of arranging their own programmes of music, "à la carte", you might say.

Gabriel Fauré was delighted to be able to "hear himself", conducting his works himself: the Suite from *Pelléas et Mélisande, Shylock,* the *Élégie* for 'cello, or the *Romance* for violin that he transcribed for piano under the title *Troisième Romance sans Paroles.*

I was often at the piano, exhausting my concert repertoire, and tirelessly playing his piano works, which included, of course, the *Ballade.* Fauré had just finished the *Ninth Nocturne,* the "Venetian Nocturne", as Joseph de Marliave called it.

One evening, when Fauré was standing by me, I played him this *Barcarolle* once, twice . . . "If it doesn't put you out," he said to me pleasantly, "I would really love to hear it one more time." How could I refuse? The bewitching music rang out again.

Lugano was a happy place for Fauré to work at his composition. It was there, too, that, between two scenes of *Pénélope,* he composed the *Fifth Impromptu* for piano.

Dear Florent Schmitt, did you ever know that you were responsible for this work, as I shall explain later? You would no doubt have commented on this with one of your habitual flashes of caustic wit.

One day a friend announced to him the appointment of Roger Ducasse as Inspector of Music at the Ville de Paris. Jean Cruppi, who was Minister at the time, had this happy idea: "It is a position which will help him to support his heavy responsibility" — alluding to Ducasse's two sisters who lived with him. Florent Schmitt replied: "You call them heavy? They don't weigh fifty kilos between them!"

Another example of his dry repartee accured when he had dropped his pince-nez at the Opéra. A lady there dived to the floor and busied herself with looking for it with the words: "But, Maître, we would certainly have heard it fall."

"What, Madame, don't you know the acoustics of the Opéra, then?"

Behind this wit, as under the tunic of Nessus, he hid the distress that is the creator's lot, and which is so very painful to express. When in 1958, very old and ailing, Florent Schmitt was in Strasbourg at the première of his *Symphony,* during the applause he leaned towards René Dumesnil, the important critic of *Le Monde,* from whom I heard this story, and said to him: "Well, this isn't the music of a dying man, is it?" Since then, alas, he has left us, but as long as his memory remains in the hearts of his friends, the splendour of his work confers immortality upon him.

The amount of Fauré in my repertoire was growing, as did the desire within me to give this grand recital. I used to think that my development would entail other allegiances; at the beginning of my career I had not been the devotee of Fauré that I had since become, attracted by the beauty that I discovered by working on the music. I was well aware of the boldness of such a performance which had been attempted by no-one before me.

My programme had been arranged, and I launched myself into this marvellous adventure, aware of my audacity and of the risk I ran with such a programme: the *Theme and Variations,* three *Nocturnes,* five *Barcarolles,* five *Impromptus,* three *Valses-Caprices* and, to end, the *Ballade,* for which I was accompanied on the second piano by the composer.

Three works were receiving their first performances: the *Fourth Impromptu,* which Fauré had dedicated to me, the *Fifth Impromptu,* "amusing and quite new, with a very curious whole-tone descent at its end", and the sublime *Ninth Barcarolle.*

On the evening itself, my quite understandable stage-fright grew with the fear that I might disappoint Fauré. I felt that he, too, was quite nervous about this evening, wished for, waited for — and feared.

I had to succeed, to win, and, in a word, once more: face things.

The audience in the Salle Érard was fairly large, attracted by the personality of the composer, by his position of Director of the Conservatoire, and, let us admit it, by curiosity. All sorts of feelings were mixed together in our audience: benevolence and hostility, as with those "première audiences" that are prepared to react in different ways.

The peak of my happiness came when, going for one final rehearsal in the afternoon on the piano which was already in place on the platform, I met Maître Louis Diémer, who asked me carelessly: "But aren't you going to play the whole from memory?" I felt my courage fail, because I had not thought about this. I had goose pimples, and was suddenly aware of the cruel difficulties of memorising Fauré's music.

To get everything in order, just before the concert, I was doing some finger exercises in the green room at the Salle Érard, when I was visited by the famous Delaborde (I knew that all my colleagues and professors at the Conservatoire were on the watch for any sagging of resolve!) who could find nothing better to say than this hardly comforting observation: "But, my little Margot, are you playing all that by heart?" Never had that phrase, "by heart", so obscure in its origins, seemed to me so laden with meaning.

Indeed, things didn't improve. When the usher opened the doors to the stage — I nearly wrote "ring" — I was so het up that I had to run back to have one last look at my music: I felt that I didn't know how the first piece began.

But finally, as usual, the miracle happened.

As I walked determinedly on to the platform, I saw sitting in the front row of seats, right at the foot of the piano, the great, blind organist, Louis Vierne, that marvellous musician whom I knew to be a devoted admirer of Fauré. His presence comforted me. The "hurdle" had been overcome. I was freed from the grip of fear. On that evening Vierne's presence was the catalyst for my energy.

Nocturnes, Barcarolles and Valses followed in the same spirit of love and enthusiasm. The hardest part was over, successfully.

Gabriel Fauré, a happy man, simply said to me his usual phrase, as he had on the day of the première of the *Ballade* at the Société des Concerts du Conservatoire, "That is something realised for me". That was my reward, for I would have been very upset if Fauré had not been completely satisfied.

Who knows how many times since then have Vierne and I recalled that recital, and the good that his presence did me? I was delighted, too, to have the opportunity to play at the Société Nationale in the première of his *Sonata for Piano and 'Cello* with real success. Stamped with the mark of Fauré, it is a magnificent work which we don't hear often enough.

Let me add here that I was very proud, with this first recital of Gabriel Fauré, to have given the lie explicitly to the preconceived notion that his music does not impress an audience, and this not through the use of effects, which Fauré considered "the worst thing of all", but by inspiring respect through its fullness.

7 The friends of Fauré

What a marvellous character Isaac Albéniz was. His exceptional, dazzling nature made him capable of great enthusiasms as well as of acts of surprising thoughtlessness. He adored his wife and forgot all about her one day in London...

His dedications, inscribed on his works, bear witness, through their overblown expressiveness, to his generous nature. He used to laugh at it himself, and told me: "I have to show that I am Spanish." He was unable to resist his desires, and was quite prepared to compromise his material well-being to satisfy them.

He was twenty years old, studying music in Belgium on a grant from his government, when he met Liszt, heard him, was tremendously excited by his music, and did not hesitate to abandon everything to follow him. His admiration for Fauré was just as great as that felt by Liszt for Wagner, and he used every ounce of his energy to organise at Barcelona concerts dedicated to the works of the man he considered to be the purest of French musicians. Kindness and devotion were familiar aspects of Albéniz's character. I need no more proof than this tale which is not well enough known and which I am happy to tell here because it is a striking illustration of his touching big-heartedness.

Isaac Albéniz and Ernest Chausson were very close friends. The latter's considerable fortune damaged his professional career as a composer. Publishers would not agree to bring out his works except "at the composer's expense". This he found humiliating — it pained him to be thought of as an amateur.

Albéniz, who was a prodigious pianist, used the excuse of a concert tour of Germany to ask his friend to entrust to him the manuscript of the *Poéme for violin and orchestra* which he considered a masterpiece. He made certain of its publication at his own expense, and on his return, claiming that it was from the publisher, gave Ernest Chausson his first copyright. Chausson never knew the truth.

Albéniz was indeed a man of great feeling. He worshipped Gabriel Fauré, and I can say, in all fairness, that he died with his music in his heart. We were intimate friends with this Spanish composer and went to see him almost every evening up to the end of his life. His opera *Pepita Jimenez* was translated into French by my husband. I would sit down at the piano and he would have me play over all his music, even works of his youth, and as we played through them he would destroy those with which he was no longer pleased.

I shall always remember our last visit to him. It was a Sunday, and that afternoon I had been playing at the Concerts Colonne. Albéniz was leaving the next day for Cambo, where he was to die shortly afterwards. Gabriel Fauré and Paul Dukas were at his side. So as not to lose a moment of the precious time left to us to spend with our friend, I was still wearing my concert dress, whose whiteness contrasted sharply with the infinite sadness pervading the room.

Albéniz, who was as thin as a skeleton, was lifted up, huddled in an enormous, rough dressing-gown. He said to me: "Marguerite, play me Fauré's *Second Valse-Caprice*. Dukas is very fond of it, too." You can guess with how much feeling I sat down at the piano. The atmosphere was oppressive. In the middle of the piece, Albéniz, who was sitting beside me, flung himself on my shoulder and sobbed: "It's all over for me. I won't hear this divine music played any more."

He left unfinished *Navarra*, that colourful and rhythmical masterpiece that he wrote for me when he was at death's door. Déodat de Séverac finished it with the tactful respect for his teacher and friend which only a great artist can bring to such a hallowed task. I have never been able to play it, but God knows how many times I have had my pupils work on it, always with great feeling. The contrast between this ardent, passionate music and the proximity of death is dramatic indeed.

Albéniz did not intend *Navarra* to be a separate piece. He

had spoken to me of a suite in the spirit of *Ibéria*, requiring great virtuosity; or at least I presume so, because Albéniz had said to me with his usual humour: "You know, you are going to have to eat steak to play this!" Alas, it was not to be.

Right up till his last days he took great care to bring about performances of the music of those he loved. It was in 1908, at the end of his life, that he organised a Fauré Festival in Barcelona. Three concerts were intended: a piano recital, a concert of chamber music and an orchestral concert. I was due to take part in each of them.

How were the Spanish audiences, raised to *Zarzuelas*, knowing only the marked rhythms of typical works as colourful as the dances and songs of Spain, going not only to receive but to understand Fauré's music, imbued with the subtle fragrance of France? Would the attraction of opposites allow them to enjoy its touching sensitivity?

Doubtless they would, since at the concert, eager to show their approval, they did not wait for the end of the *Theme and Variations* which I was playing, and applauded the brilliant second-last variation, which provoked whispered hushing from the rows of the few "initiates", who for their part were waiting for the triumphant major which brightens the end of this heavenly work.

Two days later the orchestral concert took place. The *Ballade* was on the programme, and Gabriel Fauré was to conduct it. Like many great composers, he was a terrible conductor, listening without conducting. We nearly ran into disaster with an orchestra which did not know the work. This meant that I really had to concentrate. His customary lack of control was heightened by his preoccupation with his election to the Institut Français which was taking place that very day. The death of Reyer had left a place vacant.

Gabriel Fauré, as director of the Conservatoire, did not have to worry about failure, but in the person of Charles-Marie Widor he had a fearsome rival who was pulling all the powerful strings he knew. And still more, his enemies, set dead against him, were attempting the impossible to prevent him being elected.

The campaign had been lively, led, happily, by Camille

Saint-Saëns, who had hastily returned from Algeria, and by Frémiet, Fauré's father-in-law, who had the ear of his colleagues, the painters and sculptors. Massenet, who was ill, remained aloof and declared himself in favour only at the last minute. It was a close fight. Five ballots were necessary before Fauré's election could be announced. But we were in Barcelona all this time.

The rehearsal of the concert began at eight o'clock in the evening. My husband was on the watch at the hotel, waiting for a message which he would bring to us immediately. Fauré, at the conductor's desk, kept looking at me all the time, not to conduct his work, but impatient for news of events. In the immense hall of the Liceo, which can hold an audience of seven thousand, my eyes were fixed on the door.

At the end of the rehearsal, after midnight, Fauré, who still had not heard anything, wanted to catch up with the news. At the Post Office we learned that a strike had paralysed all lines of communication. Very exasperated, Fauré told us that if he did not know anything by morning he would cancel the dinner to be given in his honour. We persuaded him to be patient yet and went our separate ways in the middle of the night.

At dawn, while we were enjoying a much-needed sleep, Fauré knocked at the door, brandishing the message: he had been appointed. Life resumed its usual course and naturally the dinner took place.

THE SOCIETY OF FRIENDS OF GABRIEL FAURÉ

"S'il etait vrai que l'on ne peut convaincre que les convertis, ce serait à désespérer",[1] Georges Duhamel has written. I agree with him that one must never weary of spreading the good word and leading unbelievers towards the paths of truth. There is no limit to this long crusade in support of Fauré's work.

One day in 1935, with my dear friend Germaine de Jouvenel, a musician and a dedicated admirer of Fauré, we

---

[1] "If It were true that one can convince only the converted, it would drive one to despair."

were deploring the fact that Gabriel Fauré's music was still so neglected. We were very worried to think of the uncertain future, which would be the fate of masterpieces, if the torch were no longer carried.

Henry de Jouvenel, who was then with the Government, said to us with his air of busy authority: "Well, if you do something for this great master instead of all these lamentations, I shall help you." The idea had just been born. Sometime afterwards the Society of Friends of Gabriel Fauré was founded. Our aim was not only to honour the genius of the composer of *Pénélope*, but to assure the most effective diffusion of his work possible, either by instituting a Gabriel Fauré Competition or by supporting concerts and festivals dedicated to his music.

The committee was formed by Madame Henry de Jouvenel. She assumed the presidency and entrusted me with the vice-presidency. Henry de Jouvenel, then *Président de l'Action artistique*, appointed his director there, Robert Brussel, organiser of the new society which grouped together all those who had served the cause of Fauré's music.

On the 28th May 1935, a most impressive demonstration, under the aegis of the Society of Friends of Gabriel Fauré, took place at the Opéra. Philippe Gaubert conducted the orchestra of the Société des Concerts du Conservatoire.

This outstanding programme of the festival deserves to be remembered. It included the *Requiem* with Ninon Vallin and Charles Panzéra, the *Madrigal* with the combined voices of Ninon Vallin, Germaine Cernay, José de Trévi and Charles Panzéra. I played the *Ballade*, then as an encore the *Second Impromptu*; then in the second part came the *Orchestral Suite from Shylock*, comprising an *Epithalame*, *Nocturne* and *Finale*. Finally there was the *Prélude* and the entire second act of *Pénélope* with Germaine Lubin, Germaine Cernay, José de Trévi and Martial Singher.

All these great names in music had come together for this first act of homage paid to the memory of the great musician since his death in 1924. To assure continuity and to induce standards in young artists that would help increase acquaintance with his work the idea of a competition came to mind.

But cruel destiny was on the look-out. That big-hearted

man, Henry de Jouvenel, died in October 1935. Deprived of its driving force, the Society's activities were suspended. But I, alas, knew of the pacifying power of music on grief, and I prevailed upon my friend, Madame de Jouvenel, to revive the Society of Friends of Gabriel Fauré. The project of the competition was taken up again.

The years 1937, 1938 and 1939 were each marked by one of these competitions. The first was a piano competition with the *Sixth Nocturne* as the test piece. The second was devoted to the songs; any could be chosen for the first test, but for the finale the choice was between *Nell*, *Clair de Lune*, *Automne*, *Au Cimitière* and *Soir*, according to the tessitura of the voices. For the third competition the *First Sonata for Piano and Violin* was required. Among the winners, the name of Jean Doyen still stands out as a great interpreter of Fauré.

Stimulated by the growing interest that these competitions offered, and on the instigation of Louis Aubert, a faithful pupil of Fauré and a member of the Society, Luxemburg Radio decided to support our activity. From the 25-27th April 1939 the Gabriel Fauré Competition took place at Luxemburg, under the illustrious patronage of Her Royal Highness The Grand Duchess and the auspices of the Grand Ducal Government, and, of course, with the agreement of the Society of Friends of Gabriel Fauré. It was endowed with important prizes and brought together an international jury under the presidency of Richard Strauss and Emil Sauer. The programme was comprised of the *Fourth Nocturne* and the *Second Impromptu* for solo piano for the first examination, and the *Ballade* with orchestra for the final one.

This was a fine opportunity to sound out the opinion of the great musicians on the jury which had just awarded the Grand Prix to a young Hungarian, H. Farago. At the concert given for the presentation of the prizes, Richard Strauss, the president of the Competition, came to me after the performance of the *Suite from Shylock* and, visibly moved, said to me: "How can it be that I did not know a work like that? I am bowled over by what I have heard." This master of descriptive music felt the receptive charm of Fauré's inspiration through that affinity which unites souls.

(Richard Strauss also had a presentiment of the secrets

from beyond. Coming out of a coma, he had said to his son: "*Death and Transfiguration* [one of his most beautiful symphonic poems]... Yes, it is just that". Then his eyes closed for ever).

That same evening in 1939, my friend Emil Sauer, the president of the jury, for whom also Fauré's music had been a revelation, said to me: "Who is this great musician? I know his name certainly, but only now have I discovered his music."

Edited under the aegis of the Society of Friends of Gabriel Fauré, Vladimir Jankélévich's book bears witness to our activity.

I remained true to our wish to raise every year a monument in sound to Fauré's glory (which is, after all, what the Festivals did) and was joined at the Palais de Chaillot on the 12th March 1939 by Charles Münch who revived *Prométhée*, led the *Ballade* to one of its henceforth habitual triumphs, and gave an unforgettable performance of the *Requiem*.

On the 3rd May 1940, when threatening clouds were darkening the horizon, we gave once more, for the benefit of the Conservatoire canteen, a concert of chamber music, with the two *Piano Quartets*, *L'Horizon Chimérique*, and the *Elégie*. My heart beats faster when I think of that evening: Jacques Thibaud was there, Maurice Vieux, Maurice Maréchal, Charles Panzéra, Louis Aubert.

Some days later came the great dispersal, the exodus, the end of an era, and in this torment, the Society was laid to rest.

8 The enchanted circle

The superiority of the art of Gabriel Fauré stems from its respect for the law of the three unities. This is one of the characteristics of authentic classicism.

First there is the *unity of style*, which is the perfect homogeneity of musical language and the consistency of the personality throughout the work. It is this, too, that allows us to recognise a page of Fauré from its first bars, as a familiar voice reveals itself.

The *unity of rhythm* is the persistence, obvious or subtle, of one basic rhythm despite the rhythmic variety of the entire work. This pulse is life itself in a work. If used with delicacy, this persistence avoids the reproach of obsessiveness which is even less tolerable than that of unchanging tonality.

Finally, *tonal unity* enjoys the variety of modulations, where Fauré discovers the most subtle nuances.

Harmonic change was never for him an end in itself, but a means of seduction, whether he used it to affect swift changes in his harmonic plans or whether it plunged his caressing melodies into a period of indecision which makes their gentle, undulating charm even more sensitive.

In the middle of all this diversity Fauré always observed tonal unity despite the boldness of his surprising writing. When he leaves the principal key, the departure seems logical and necessary. He had a marvellous harmonic instinct and moved with ease between the most varied of keys which he always linked most exquisitely. Often, when he had come to the most distant key, he would return, by some supple volte-face in his writing, to his original key by the shortest route, the most unexpected, sometimes the most picturesque, thus declaring with force the unity of the work. There was no dogmatism in this strict observance of the rule and his hand was always guided by his imagination and his sensitivity.

Fauré's classicism is derived entirely from instinct and spontaneity rediscovered in re-creating the truth of the classical spirit, thoroughly imbued with that sense of realism that requires one to accept material constraint and not to do violence to the means one has chosen. It is in this magisterial docility, indeed, in this probity that I see the reason that makes Fauré's piano music so well suited to the instrument.

But here I must diverge, because if Fauré is perhaps the greatest of our musical poets, if his piano music speaks from the heart in the sense of mind or of soul, if he touches us with the most sensitive of messages, if he attracts us with the spell of his charm, one must admit that this music is very hard to play, requiring a technique free from all pianistic shortcomings, with extreme independence of the fingers and of nuance too, and thorough knowledge of the sounds that one can draw from the instrument. The music is certainly not made to show off the skills it requires from those who play it.

No music conceals better the difficulties of its demands. Some derive from clumsiness in the writing, which can make it more difficult to play than much of Liszt's transcendental music which fits more easily under the fingers of the pianist. What makes Fauré's music difficult to play is its moving, distracting character, which is required to carry his phrasing, his superimposed voices and his changes of time signature.

This "pianism", which is very characteristic for those who have got to know it, derives from music which has been intended, required for the piano, and indeed it is for the piano that Fauré wrote some of his greatest masterpieces. Through him, playing the instrument transforms itself into a wealth of discoveries in sound, springing from the imagination as one touches the piano. Shimmering, fluid, iridescent arpeggios by prolonging the sound with the pedals or combining the vibrations allowed by both pedals, he can vary his effects infinitely. This technique is so well adapted to the resources of the piano that any orchestral transcription is quite unthinkable.

THERE ARE NOT TYPES OF MUSIC,
THERE IS JUST MUSIC

Fauré's music is at the same time sensual and spare; sensual because of its sonority, its depth, indeed the voluptuousness of the writing; spare because it evokes no story, no picture. Thus the musical idea gushes forth and the source of the inspiration remains pure music "of the first voice".

Drawn from the depths of artistic sensitivity, the imagination has created a sound picture directly, without using any idea which would have enclosed it in too strict a formula. Nocturnes, Barcarolles, Impromptus, Valses: all these terms indicate a *genre*. Fauré once more agreed with Verlaine: "Music before everything". Held back by an instinctive shyness, his music no more reflected the sentiments than the sensations of its composer. His inspiration takes the shape of a discreet and refined secret which is now lost. Since Fauré, it seems that we have passed the limits of aesthetic form without being able to find again what makes his œuvre so profoundly and exquisitely delicate. Yet how many inventions and how many discoveries do we have, thanks to his activity, and which have been carried off by so many others to be used to their profit? But his preoccupation when writing them was not novelty. They are the consequence of the master's musical organisation, one of the most sensitive and sharpest that existed, and not the result of his will. They are the means, not the end: the means to enhance a musical idea, to make it more expressive, and not a goal in itself.

A superior quality can always be found in Fauré's handling of form; he was able to bend traditional writing to the most refined expression of taste, all the while respecting the demands of pure classical discipline.

Gabriel Fauré, who was quite at home with matters of paradox, I often found rather disconcerting. I was quite sure that if one wanted to play a work one had to know its sources, and I would ask him about the birth of an idea or a theme: he would give some flippant answer. Once, when I was going into raptures about the beauty of the theme of the *Sixth Nocturne*, which he wrote during a stay at a friend's home, I said to him: "That must be very lovely". He laughed and answered: "You'll never guess where I thought of it!" And, indeed, I had to admit that there was no link between his poetic inspiration and the place where it had occurred to him!

That was perhaps his way of hiding the secrets of the creative artist. Maurice Ravel, indeed, said: "And if I want to be artificial...", but this just proves once more that Fauré's music finds its *raison d'être* in itself alone.

Nevertheless, there is nothing enigmatic in what Fauré is trying to say. I believe, quite simply, that to decipher its meaning, one must first be in full control of one's technical faculties. It is simply that. And now that we are at the doorstep of the œuvre, let us talk a little about its execution.

Whenever one talks about music, one must first think of the means of producing it. Now, there does exist a technique for Fauré. This music requires that one "play it straight" without camouflage or trickery. That is one of the reasons that make it seem so difficult. Without the dash and brilliance that he required of his performers, it is from his very personal approach to the keyboard, both heavy and supple, that playing Fauré derives the precise, firm and delicately tender accentuation that is needed to play his music. His rather heavy hand could produce a very lovely, rather rounded tone that fitted well "Fauré's style".

He would often say to me after he had been listening to me: "It always gives me great pleasure to hear myself played with verve. On the pretext of getting involved in the work, people always play me as if the blinds were down, just the way they think that you have no need for a voice to sing my songs."

The technique requred for Fauré is a true technique, with all the complex demands that it entails. It allows one to overcome difficulties even to the point of forgetting them. "To have fingers" is not a meaningless expression, because that is what one makes music with, and without them you cannot do anything. As I wrote in my book on the piano: it is knowledge of the *piano* that must be acquired.

One hears misused today words that I condemn: "relax" or "loosen". These are incorrect terms because they are quite

opposed to the action of playing the piano. It is enough to be
supple, you do not need to use a special word. One should
not confuse technique and the actual playing which is only
part of it. It is wrongly said of the great virtuoso: "Oh, he has
a great technique", just because he can play octaves quickly
or bend his fingers brilliantly. Technique is something completely different. It includes everything — from the movement
of fingers and wrists to the richness of the sound and use of
pedals with all the infinite ways of approaching the keyboard.

Gabriel Fauré had two maxims he was fond of and used
to repeat "six times an hour": "Nuance is the thing," he
would say, "not a change of movement". Or again: "The bass
line is with us", and it is to Fauré that I have to thank my
love of the bass line in music. How right he was. I have spent
my life demonstrating the truth of this. The entire construction is built on the bass line and without it music collapses.
Any musician worthy of the name has this respect for the
bass line. It is the root of harmony, the fundamental support
of the chord. It must always be laid down, without heaviness,
of course, but with sufficient strength to balance the phrase
it supports. It is the rallying point which assures stability
of the formation of successive modulations.

At one of the big concerts given at the Institut, Charles-
Marie Widor, who was then Permanent Secretary, asked me to
play some of Fauré's music. While I was playing, Widor had
his eyes closed and I even thought that he was asleep. As the
last note died away, he sat up and said: "Oh, what a lovely
bass line". Some months later the great organist underwent
an operation for cataracts. I wrote to him offering my wishes
for a speedy recovery and as a post-script to his answer he
added: "And that lovely bass line — I think of it yet".

ON THE NUANCES

The unintelligibility of any interpretation always derives
from being played "with the same colour". It is shading that
gives variety. There is a great deal to be said on this subject,
one of the most delicate questions posed by playing. Of
course one must respect the requirements indicated by the
composer. Nevertheless, it often happened, with Fauré beside

me, that I had to differ from what was written. This would be quite impossible with Claude Debussy or Maurice Ravel, who were orchestrators, a thing Gabriel Fauré was not. We knew that he was always assisted by his pupils for his orchestration of *Pénélope*. Fauré's phrasing was very long, his perorations endless (Debussy said: "He doesn't know how to finish"), and these required support from variety in shading. I tried to make his phrasing more striking, to enhance the value of a dynamic, to find inflections which were not accentuated, but which gave the right kind of sound to a modulation. After I had considered the effect for a long time beforehand, I would submit my proposals to the master for his approval.

I worked with him from 1902–1912, and during these years the validity of the interpretation of so many of his works firmly established itself with us. It is this that I pass on today, because its validity has been testified by Fauré himself. He would often say to me after one of our working sessions that he had "just made a discovery about his music", and I knew that after this he would require from others playing his music just what we had realised together.

He liked crescendo and diminuendo to be short and effective, just like Toscanini, who obtained in this way the most striking effects of his staggering dynamism. Fauré had adopted the rule for shading that Hans von Bülow had laid down: when one reads "crescendo", it means leaving a more "piano" tone for a reinforcement of the sound; and when one reads "diminuendo", it indicates that one is playing as loudly as one can to allow the tone to be softened.

ON STYLE

"And I always enjoy seeing sunlight play on the rocks, the water, the trees and plains. What variety of effects, what brilliance and what softness... I wish my music could show as much diversity."[1] In this letter of Fauré's one finds the echo of the style that his music requires. Brilliance and

---

[1] From a private letter.

softness of phrasing and transparency of sound with absolute precision of touch.

Rubato in Fauré is close to Chopin, and derives from freedom in the rounding of the phrase and respect for the underlying pace. One must never forget, and I repeat this, that Gabriel Fauré thought that the search for effect was the worst sin of all. He said, and rightly, that Beethoven's technique was not Liszt's, and I would say in my turn that Fauré's is not Debussy's, but the chain of tradition which links the one with the other is still the safest path for us players. Playing Fauré is different from playing Debussy, for whom every note is a sound, whence the necessity of as varied a tonal palette as possible; while with Fauré it is the line that counts. For one, a series of sounds; for the other, a line of different timbres.

As a general rule, one must consider simple, short notes, or in octaves, as part of an expressive, melodic line with a meaning as distinct as the long note which follows. Imagine you have a word which corresponds to a note in a vocal melody: you would have to pronounce it — "make the note speak" is not a meaningless metaphor. I would like everyone to know that you cannot take liberties with music. It is the negation of style which debases playing. The style depends on technique because, without a technique suitable to the demands of a particular work, you can offer no interpretation.

Fauré, who showed such indifference in other matters, had adopted an attitude of real "musical tyranny" when it came to style. In fact, one might say that I was shared between him and my husband. One morning, when I had rehearsed the *Third Concerto* of Beethoven at the Concerts Lamoureux, in the presence of my two "musical advisors", we went home in a cab. It was quite a distance from the Théâtre Sarah-Bernhardt. I felt that Fauré, who wasn't saying a word, was in a bad mood. "Well, what is the matter, Maître? Did I play badly?" He answered grumpily: "Why did you play the last passage in the cadence of the last movement with two hands? Beethoven's technique is not that of Liszt." "I told her so," my husband said. "When you have such a musician to hand, you listen to him," Fauré said, going one better.

To put an end to it I said brusquely: "Alright, there is no

need to make such a fuss about it. I'll change the passage on Sunday." "And you'll make a mess of it," Fauré added. "I hope not, all the same," I said, exasperated. When I was back home I worked on the offending passage, and the next day I played it impeccably with my right hand triumphant.

Camille Chevillard, who had conducted the concerto, came to the right conclusion in the matter without knowing it. "You changed the way you played that passage," he said characteristically, "and you were right. The other way wasn't worthy of you." I relate this anecdote that it might serve as an example to our young musicians who too often take annoying liberties with scores.

There is another passage which illustrates the respect in which Fauré held the style of the great classics. It was examination day at the Conservatoire. We had given each other the cold shoulder and exchanged neither word nor glance. One of my pupils (at the time I was in charge of a keyboard class) took the advice of a professor of a superior class in which she hoped to enrol and decided to use two hands to play a passage in Mozart. André Messager, who was on the jury, witnessed Fauré's violent reaction and the thunderous look he threw at me. I parried the blow immediately by saying, loud enough to be heard by the director, "You can well imagine it wasn't me who told her to do that." "It didn't prevent me from thinking he was going to speak to you," Messager said as we left the competition.

We were actually going through an evaluation of piano technique which, put to the service of certain percussive pieces of music, entails the danger of compromising the qualities required to play Fauré. Depth of tone in the suppleness of the *attacca*, equal agility in the fingers (that famous soaring over the keyboard), rapid, winged playing which characterises the technique required for Fauré, just as for Chopin.

ON WORKING

To make anything of a career, one must first start it off. Before one arrives one bothers less about it. It first requires work, love and much humility.

By working up to the last minute before a concert, I have always felt better able to bring life to the music I was to play. To make constant progress, which is very necessary, dissatisfaction is profitable. Put the piece on the piano a hundred times — that, believe me, is the secret of success. I agree with what my pupil Wayenberg said after a very successful concert: "I am happy but I am not satisfied". Much more recently, one of the great pianists of the day, after a triumphant recital, shut himself away in his studio to play the material over again until five o' clock in the morning; he was perhaps the only one not to have liked his own interpretation.

Our elders preached by example; my old friend Francis Planté had, one afternoon, shut himself away to work. One of his old fellow-pupils came to see him, but ran up against this self-imposed confinement. He returned in the evening and was much surprised to hear Planté tirelessly repeating the same difficult passage. I have in my files a card from Planté signed "The schoolboy still plodding away in his 97th year". Meditation on these examples benefit many young pianists who want to run before they can walk. The greatest are fierce workers. It was at Évian that I met Vladimir Horowitz. "What a shame I'm leaving tomorrow," I told him. "I'm not sorry you're leaving," he answered. "I came here to work on Chopin's *B Minor Sonata* and I have rented a house for three months."

Our art needs a great deal of patience. Above all one must not believe ceaseless effort is in vain or will go unnoticed.

I still remember the *Concerto in F* of Chopin that Messager had orchestrated for me. At the rehearsal I still had not played the main theme to my satisfaction. In the afternoon I went to Érard, who had prepared the concert piano, and spent hours seeking the right way to play the theme. The next day at the concert it was better.

In Claude Debussy's *Fantaisie*, the first phrase of the *Andante* just would not come right. I had tried it a hundred times, and between two performances I was very pleased to hear Messager say: "You have been working on this".

Nonetheless, the paradoxes in Fauré sometimes bewildered me. Despite his very great respect for tradition, he was much less intransigent when it came to his own compositions. He could even be disconcerting. During a rehearsal of one of his works, the conductor was not sure about a point in the score, so he asked Fauré, who replied apathetically: "Well, I don't really know". One day, arriving at my house unexpectedly, he found me at the piano, playing his *Theme and Variations*, which had just been given as a competition-piece at the Conservatoire, of which he was then Director. I said to him: "Will you let the ascending passage in the second-last variation be played in octaves?" "Oh no," he said, "not in octaves. I forbid it. I detest that." Nonetheless, on the day of the competition he allowed it. Why? Because at heart he did not care. For him his work was like a bottle in the sea. He had other points in common with Alfred de Vigny: a patrician turn of mind and the same indifference to the work once it had been completed.

THE PERFORMER

To play a piece of music is to recreate it. Music — art in movement — is a construction in the spirit of the time which writing down crystallises and which playing animates. However perfectly music may be written, however scrupulously the composer has indicated his intentions, the work remains a dead letter without someone to play it. Our role is heavy with responsibility.

We should remain humble in front of a masterpiece, we should be well aware of what we do when the word 'métier' assumes its highest meaning. Musical instinct, which is so necessary, can only externalise itself if one knows one's 'métier' perfectly. It is a word that is often disparaged, but one of the loveliest I know. It is at this price that our sensitivity, indeed our personality, acquires the right to assume the marvellous task incumbent on us.

As Debussy wrote to Messager one day, the internal rhythm of all music depends on who is playing it, just as every word depends on the mouth that is speaking it. I need no further definition of the work of the interpreter.

THE METRONOME

This little instrument is doubtless necessary, but quite formidable. It almost seems a paradox to indicate a movement with a metronome number. It would seem that to understand a work would be enough to discover its meaning. There should be sufficient suppleness in the fluctuation of the phrasing, a thing which wavers, that it is impossible to advise inexorable rigidity throughout a piece by marking the time. Nevertheless, in many cases it is useful to determine the character of a piece and a metronome indication can be a control, as long as it only has relative value.

I would then advise great caution with the metronome markings in Fauré's published works. Most of them are wrong for quite a simple reason of timing: Fauré almost never had the opportunity of hearing his piano pieces played by a virtuoso before they were published, and we know well the influence that hearing a piece can have on its composer. My personal experience allows me to confirm this. All composers are inclined to re-think their works and their tempi (even though they might not want to admit it) when they have heard them played.

ON MEMORISING

There are several sorts of memory: aural memory, which has the ear as guide; visual memory, which can follow the score with one's eyes closed, which allows one to know where one is when one feels a shiver of fear coming on; finally, there is memory of the fingers, which is the least reliable. As the famous Marmontel used to say: "The fingers are little horses which return to the stable all on their own." I think all three are necessary.

In any case, one should learn a piece by heart immediately, but one should always work at the music so as not to get too far from the score. Memory is above all a question of attention. It is difficult to memorise Fauré's music. One little thing, one speck of dust on the piano, and one runs the risk of going off at a tangent without being able to find one's place again in the network of phrases, both precise and chimerical.

It was in working on Fauré's music that I realised that memory could hold some disagreeable surprises. Again, it was almost always a thorough knowledge of the bass line which comes to our rescue... and good luck too, as in everything else.

ON MASTERY

Mastery is self-acquired and it happens often. One must retain one's self-control in all circumstances. To dominate an audience one must first of all dominate oneself. In sum, it is a question of "taming", of keeping one's self-control and lucidity. Here again, "face things" was my shield before life.

In a word, one must never lose control of the pedals. This reminds me of a true story. I was playing one of Chopin's concertos at the Concerts Colonne one Sunday when I noticed to my annoyance that the lyre of the pedals had been broken, probably when the piano was being rolled to the front of the platform. So I played the opening *Allegro*, then had the technician called. From under the piano he whispered: "The mechanism is broken, so I will try to put in a makeshift lead." During the *Andante* it fell out under my feet. What could I do — interrupt the concert or go on? I opted for the latter solution and in the finale called on all the resources of my piano technique.

It was a great success, but did the audience notice this *tour de force*? I never knew. To play a Chopin concerto "hands only", without pedals! That day I really appreciated the necessity of having complete mastery.

ON STAGE FRIGHT

This can be a fearsome thing. One must not play with it but in spite of it, or, to put it another way, one must be strong enough to overcome it. This is not always easy.

I wonder occasionally what drives some amateur players who, although "frightened to death", still want to be heard.

There was a charming society singer, Madame X, who was so frightened before singing that she used a hot-water-bottle under her feet and took a whole arsenal of capsules. One day I asked her, a little maliciously, I admit, "But, chére Madame, I am forced to play the piano since it is my career, but why do you sing in public if it makes you so ill?" She quickly replied with a smile: "I enjoy it". Stage fright, it is true, is like love-sickness: it is quickly forgotten.

There are two sorts of stage fright. There is the kind that paralyses you, and in this case you might as well change jobs; and there is the kind which allows you to come out of yourself and which passes after you have played your first note.

Intense training too can arm you against stage fright. Madame Montigny-Rémaury, a pianist of some repute and the sister-in-law of Ambroise Thomas and contemporary of Saint-Saëns and Gabriel Fauré, and like him from Ariège, told me that she used to rehearse her concert programmes in an evening gown in her living room, the grand piano open in front of rows of cushioned chairs, with all the usual ceremony but devoid of listeners.

The artist on the platform is often a split personality. All goes well as long as one knows that "the other one" is obeying you. It is an odd yet desirable sensation. Happily this occurs often enough to make the career of the player the loveliest of all, even though it is also the most formidable.

9 The sources of Fauré's inspiration

Gabriel Fauré, repeating a thought he had often expressed to me, wrote in a letter on the 2nd August 1910: "In piano music one cannot use padding; one must pay in cash so that it is interesting all the time. It is perhaps the most difficult genre if you want to be as satisfying as possible," and he added modestly, "and I do my best". Then, as if in reply to some unjust reproach, he concluded: "Only it cannot be done any faster". For him it was always a struggle against time which had been so strictly measured out to him.

I leave to others the task of writing an epilogue on "the three styles of Fauré": these of his youth, his maturity and his old age, or, as Vuillermoz has put it, "the parallel styles that journeyed side by side and in the same step on the long road of his masterpieces", with which Florent Schmitt, too, agreed. My personal preference is for the works he wrote before the trials of deafness afflicted his hearing, those works bubbling with vitality, with emotion and with life, which I came to know at the composer's side. It seemed to me that later his creative rhythm slowed down as it began to crystallise, and that his music became starker, more deliberate and lost its divine spontaneity.

In truth, Gabriel Fauré's output for piano can be summed up in several sections:
Music of water: the *13 Barcarolles*;
Music of night: the *13 Nocturnes*;
Music of fantasy: the *4 Valses-Caprices*, the *5 Impromptus*, the *Ballade*, and *Dolly*;
Music of reason: the *Theme and Variations* and the

several Preludes and Fugues which are dotted about his oeuvre.

There is a wealth of songs, so marvellously rich, some chamber music works, and the unforgettable *Pénélope,* preceded by *Prométhée* and the divine *Requiem*, close the Enchanted Circle.

THE BLUE TONE OF THE BARCAROLLES

The *Barcarolles* are certainly the most characteristic compositions of Fauré's genius; the undulating flexibility of his subtle art accords happily with the character of the piece, and his rhythmic invention is extraordinary. The persistence of one rhythm requires great sense of touch, because quite often its obsessiveness is less tolerable than remaining in a single key. The second subject in the *Barcarolles* is always rhythmically related to the first — and no monotony ever results from it.

These *Barcarolles* are emotive states, they are states of the soul of a musician-poet whose tradition and taste draw us towards the serene beauty of southern seas. It is truly there that we find the "midi" in music. The divine clarity of Latin seas, the voluptuousness, now smiling, now serious, and their wholesome langour, too, breathe again in these delightful poems: for water is but the tears and the blood of the earth. Who will sing more beautifully of the poetry of springs, the ballad of water awake or asleep, its sparkle, its colours, and the faces mirrored there, disincarnate in their transparence; and who will better tell the joys they give by quenching all thirst with the softness of their caresses? "Man, like the sea, has his waves and his caprices," said the stern Boileau.

Let us examine together the *Barcarolles*, to discover their enchanted world. In the mystery of his inner silence, Gabriel Fauré perceived the equivalent in sound of fleeting or powerful impressions.

Ronsard sang of the spring that would never dry up:

> La, sont par la Nature enclose
> Au fond de cent mille vaisseaux

Les semences de toutes choses
Éternelles filles des eaux.[1]

The *First Barcarolle* sings the haunting song of the waves and the powerful song of the open sea.

Overflowing joy and childlike enthusiasm illuminate the *Second Barcarolle*, perhaps the most lyrical outpouring of his fantasy.

"The melodious and proud happiness of the vessels that sail the gentle seas," evokes the poet Louis Mercier in *L'Enchantée*.

The sad and gentle melody of the *Third Barcarolle* throws a soft shadow on the rêverie "which delicately informs the work". The melody floats as if adrift between uncertain tonalities. It gets quite lost in a delightful lapping of sounds before the return of the principal key in G flat major.

I find it quite marvellous. Its swaying rhythm, lit up with singing phrases, takes flight in the apparent freedom of the feeling that gives it life. One must play it as a thing of great poetry. I shall never forget the skill with which Blanche Selva, although not a great enthusiast of Fauré's music, played the *gruppetto* which crowns it as if it were the sea-foam on the edge of a wave.

The *Fourth* is most attractive in its satin-like balance.

The glorious *Fifth Barcarolle*, alive and powerful, smells of salt, of sea-wind and breathes a vigorous and wholesome joy. One can hear the cries of sailors, and its melody has the pace of a fishing-boat riding on the waves which comes back to square and dashes off, its sails billowing. Here I feel, like Baudelaire: "Music often takes hold of me like the sea".

---

[1] There, in Nature's confines
At the bottom of one hundred thousand vessels,
Are the seeds of all things,
Eternal daughters of the waves.

The *Sixth Barcarolle* is quite charming, its melodic line elegant, delicate, joyful, lit up with the sun, undulating gently.

Gabriel Fauré announced the composition of the *Seventh Barcarolle* as "a little piece intended for *Le Figaro* for its Christmas number... That is quite an honour," he said with irony, "because this issue will be read throughout the world." This was also the first piece he sent to Heugel, his new publisher. "There are eight lovely pages here, and I am proud that I got through them in three days," he concluded.

The *Eighth Barcarolle* is born of the morning, rich with humour and fantasy.

My preference is perhaps for that nostalgic sketch of Venice, the *Ninth Barcarolle*, one of the most beautiful. I gave its première in my 1909 recital. Gabriel Fauré wrote it at Lugano in response to his recent contract with Heugel. Here is the reflection of his vision of Venice. I would never have been able to play this *Barcarolle* if I had not lived in Venice myself.

It is very difficult to play because its monotony should not be monotonous. Its speed, *Andante moderato*, is around 66 on the metronome. As to dynamics, we wrote them down together on the manuscript.

Venice is the marvellous setting of this poem for the piano. Each of us carries within an image of Venice from a deep and vibrant soul. For me it is the *Ninth Barcarolle*. "When I look for a word to replace 'music', I can find only the word 'Venice'," wrote Friedrich Nietzsche. Fauré, too, found the right echo.

During the summer of 1913 Fauré composed his *Tenth Barcarolle*. He was under no illusion when he wrote: "As to the piece I have started, it will only be the fiftieth or more of my piano pieces that, with rare exceptions, pianists allow to pile up without playing. That has been their lot for twenty years."[1]

[1] From a private letter.

How right he was! For my part I was deeply sorry, despite our estrangement, to see with what indifference the master's work was being treated. Is it even thinkable that the exquisite *Twelfth Barcarolle*, written in 1915 at Saint-Raphaël, quite close to the place where Gounod composed *Mireille*, was never played by its dedicatee, the pianist Louis Diémer? "I composed it," said Fauré, "by licking it over like a bear does its cubs." Since no other pianist had yet included it in a programme, I gave its première to end its neglect. It was already 1920.

Fauré spoke of his *Thirteenth Barcarolle*, rather off-handedly, as "a little piano piece composed between two movements of my *Second Piano Quintet*," and while he was engaged on a work to commemorate Napoleon's centenary. He spent that summer of 1921 at Nice. With it the cycle of the Barcarolle was finished. It was Gabriel Fauré who gave them their noble titles.

NOCTURNES

The composition of the *Thirteen Nocturnes* was spread between the years 1883 and 1921. They illustrate the evolution of Fauré's style more perceptibly in the style of writing then in the depth of thought.

"Imagining is trying to formulate all one would wish to be better, all that surpasses reality." In the light of this thought, which Fauré confided, his *Nocturnes* can be seen in their true colours. By inventing this world on the edge of reality, he brought into harmony "that which was better in himself" with the desire to escape and the need for nobility that informs the creative spirit.

It is a form of the search for beauty — "the generative condition of the work of art" — the idée fixe that haunted Baudelaire and which Paul Valéry defined to other ends in *L'Ame et la Danse*, but which could as well describe the *Nocturnes* of Gabriel Fauré: "Who knows what august laws dream here, that they have taken on clear faces and that they unite in the design to show mere mortals how the real, the unreal and the intelligible can melt and merge under the power of the Muses."

This impressionism of sensation which Fauré held dear, despite his modesty, finds its expression in the fluid art of the *Nocturnes*. He uses infinite shading, a palette of sound which derives its colour from all the dreams of his imagination.

Is not the Nocturne the form that Fauré preferred to idealise his dream? There are his indefinite, indeterminate outlines, which leave in the memory the lingering emotion, the gentle trembling that one experiences sometimes when one wakes from a dream. This is the meditation that well suits the night that is the prelude to new outbursts of feeling.

The theme of night, in its mysterious caress, bears an active power that requires discretion on the part of the musician. It is an inexhaustible source of inspiration which gives life to Fauré's most beautiful masterpieces.

How does he translate his feeling of night? Solely by timbre, the expressive character of the musical phrasing and the sequence of harmonies. Here no rigour of design is called for. The Nocturne enjoys a great deal of freedom which closely embraces all vagaries of thought in the image of a dream. Frédéric Chopin immortalised the piano Nocturne; Fauré conferred on it a more exalted lyricism and a more voluptuous eloquence. All the spells of night are evoked by his pen.

Any work, however original it may be, is always connected somehow with those that have preceded it. In the evolution of musical language nothing is created; rather, everything is transformed. Here, as elsewhere, genius is that which welds a new link on to that infinite chain.

It is from Chopin that Fauré borrowed, with the title of "Nocturne", the structure of this kind of work. A melodic phrase which emerges at length (some of the themes in the *Nocturnes* take almost two pages) confers on the work its character, be it full of feeling, ardent, elegiac, poetic or melancholy. It is generally followed by one or several themes of contrasting ideas with a central episode of a more lively pace, sometimes impassioned, which forms a contrast with the calm resignation of the whole.

I always feel some scruples when it comes to sharing my personal impressions on an aesthetic level. Fauré's inspiration was such a jealously guarded secret that to keep it so he sometimes went as far as deceit. The *Nocturnes* offer us so much musical delight that it ought to be enough to listen in order to hear it, just as one breathes to be capable of feeling. Here is the secret of the pleasure of the senses, as long as one adds a little of one's soul.

We should feel joy as we open the pages of the *Nocturnes*.

The first three date from 1883, an auspicious year which also saw the publication of the *First Valse-Caprice*, the first three *Impromptus*, the *Mazurka* and the *First Barcarolle*.

Right from the beginning of the *First Nocturne* we enter a world of pure emotion, of quiet confidence and passionate ardour, of tenderness and poetry... Dark and profound, with rays of hope which are extinguished and outbursts of beauty which fall back again. The piece ends with a heart-rending cry that calls to mind the *Lament of the Sinner*. On the second page Fauré indicated a change of speed to me for, given the agitated nature of the bass line, he wanted a more rapid tempo up to the return of the first subject. It also requires that care be given to the sound when the first subject is re-introduced in octaves "like the silhouette of a shadow".

With the *Second Nocturne* the scene changes. Its intimate gentleness seems undisturbed by the agitation which reigns in its central section. Paul Dukas was especially fond of this *Nocturne*.

The delicate, crystalline sounds of the *Third Nocturne* are typical of Fauré, but the memory of Chopin can still be felt. The work is elegant and youthful, with flights of dream-like rapture and weary melancholy.

The *Fourth Nocturne* is a wonderful love-song. The poet contemplates night, his accomplice, his heart full of memories, perhaps of regrets, cries echo, the atmosphere quivers, and in the passionate night arises a hymn of exaltation. Then comes an "ecstasy of langour"; everything dies away and calm returns.

ADVICE TO PERFORMERS

It was in 1884 that Gabriel Fauré composed his *Fourth Nocturne in A flat major*, Op. 36.

When one tackles a work one must trust the character of the theme to get through first of all to the "meaning of the work". Never depart from the continuity of the musical phrase so as not to sever it, but follow it and avoid too slow a pace. The deformation of pace entails the deformation of the work.

For the *Fourth Nocturne* it is better to keep to the *Andante molto moderato*, which suggests a walking pace, without haste. I would suggest a metronome number at around ♩=66 and not the marking of ♩=56 as in the published version, which does not, I would assert, coincide with Fauré's wishes — although, of course, admitting that this is given as an indication of preference and need not be rigidly observed.

As in almost all the *Nocturnes*, the theme takes some time to reveal itself. At the fourth bar, after the rush of the triplet of quavers, which is to be played without harshness, link the phrase in the same way. For example:

The left hand, which derives its balance from the *Ballade*, is 'piano' and quite equal to the pedal on the first note of the bass line.

Bars 10 and 11: play 'portamento legato' with all the harmonies 'pianissimo'.

When the theme is repeated in octaves, the playing is intensified. (The arpeggios of the bass line should be played with their first note clearly emphasised.)

Do not exaggerate the 'piano' but on the contrary sustain the phrase as far as the modulation into E flat minor. There, based on semiquavers which should be played with a gentle 'piano', one can hear the distant chime of two notes vibrating in an atmosphere of peace. There is great tranquillity in this extended 'piano'.

While retaining this transparency of sound, one should husband the crescendo that enlivens the end of this phrase, which culminates in a warm and effusive passage of brilliance. Here, in the edition that I have in front of me, there are some serious printing errors. Bar 37:

Bars 38 and 39:

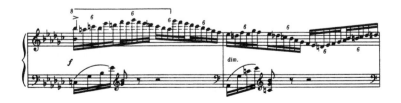

In the 39th bar, interpretation requires that one does not suppress the "sans presser" indicated; play the first phrase with warmth and then unite the D flat with the D natural between the 39th and 40th bars, where here alone is the indication 'piano' to be found.

Intensify the expression of the answers exchanged between both hands, then reduce it considerably for the 'pianissimo' return.

Gabriel Fauré was very sparing with the expression "appassionato" so as not to give it its full range. One should play here "full steam ahead", but not brutally, and follow the phrase when the left hand takes over from the right and fall lightly back the last two times before the arrival of the key of G flat major.

Retain here the gentle resounding sonority of bells and hold back considerably before the return of the 'tempo primo'. The repeat of the theme should be played with an appreciable 'rubato', with the notes which double it played a little like bells. In the 79th bar play the passage in sixths in the resonance of the chord held by the pedal. This will only be the second time that one has kept this vibration by picking out again the notes of the chord in the pedal (by depressing the keys without making them sound) and then lifting the pedal. The coda returns to the same peaceful character of the second theme, but without any 'rallentando'. Vary the colour of the four chords of the last few bars by playing a crescendo on the first three (in C minor) and play 'piano' the fourth which brings in the modulation. The conclusion is calm and very poetic: take care to play the bass of the arpeggio very 'piano', and diminuendo even more right to the end.

The *Fifth*, although from the same year, is not in the same vein. Here the two themes are very graceful. The 'cantabile' reappears most ingeniously in the tumultuous central section. There is a dawn-like freshness after the calm return.

Et dans la splendeur triste d'une lune
Se levant blafarde et solennelle une
Nuit mélancolique et lourde d'été
Pleine de silence et d'obscurité,
Berce sur l'azur qu'un vent doux effleure
L'arbre qui frissonne et l'oiseau qui pleure.[1]

Baudelaire

The *Sixth Nocturne* (1894) is the gem of the collection, one of the summits of Fauré's oeuvre, one of those masterpieces as perfect as anything music has ever produced. It is a vast poem of passion and of dreams. This *Nocturne* is pervaded by an atmosphere of intimate meditation. It is framed by a noble and serene melody which is made of two connected phrases, both dreamy and contemplative, but the second more ardently expressive. It is one of Fauré's most beautiful inspirations. From it arises a "song of great softness", hesitant and troubled at first, then more anguished. It rejoins the second part of the initial theme which brings back the delightful calm.

A new palpitating theme carried by a murmuring passage of semiquavers now takes its turn to elate. In its frenzied course it clashes with recollections of the breathless "song", and is carried with it in a passage of great pathos. Then the second phrase of the initial melody reappears transposed deep into the bass; as if overwhelmed by the force of the emotion, the melody breaks and one hears again the sublime theme of the beginning imposing its pacifying charm. The spirit of night fades into the softness of long enchantment. With the art of the magician Fauré plays with enharmonics and modulations. He slides imperceptibly from one key to another with a range of colours that an impressionist painter might envy!

---

[1] And in the sad splendour of a moon
That rises pale and solemn, a
Night that is meloncholy and heavy with summer
Full of silence and of darkness,
Rocks on the azure that a soft wind ruffles
The tree that shivers and the bird that weeps.

But, borne by words where my heart will do the speaking, here follows some advice as to interpretation.

'Adagio' gives the correct feeling of movement in this marvellous song which is developed at length.

Replace the metronome marking of 76 with 60. The theme will be shown to advantage by playing with great evenness of touch, without becoming confused by the balanced but immutable rhythm of the quaver triplets which accompany it.

Fourth bar: give a gentle inflexion to the A flat and let the D flat vibrate in both hands.

Without crushing the sound, stress the depth of the bass.

At the eighth bar do not exaggerate the 'crescendo' that is marked, but sustain the melody line before the 'diminuendo' at the end of the phrase. What follows is linked with a great unity of feeling.

12th bar:

Fauré put an accent on the first note of the bass.

Sound the E natural of bar 5 (p.2) to ensure its vibration up till the G sharp which follows it. Do not repeat it on the first beat of the next bar.

Play the octaves of the left hand very expressively. The accent of the phrase should be very sustained up to the 'fortissimo' of the third reprise, the 'diminuendo' sharp and gripping by slowing down on the last bar of this section.

The interpretation of the second theme is very difficult to explain away from the keyboard. The 'allegretto' must keep its rather agitated pace without allowing the indication 'molto moderato', which accompanies it to restrain its character. The melodic curve should be followed in the rhythm but with that rubato so special to Fauré which joins precise suppleness with palpitating freshness.

At bar 10 (p. 3) a 'crescendo' is indicated: allow the phrase to blossom into a brilliant 'fortissimo' and then extinguish it swiftly on the 'portando' descent of the fifteenth bar.

Make sure of tying the octave to the chord through finger substitution. For example, bars 34-35:

Prepare the return with the left hand before the dialogue between the two hands starts up (fifth line).

Fauré wanted a slight breathing space before the attack on the C. For example, bars 39-40:

The same holds three bars further on for the D — what follows should be played 'piano' with much charm up till the powerful crescendo which brings back the first theme with great intensity and, with a short 'diminuendo' on the modulation, to lead to an unutterably lovely end.

The 'allegro moderato' in 4/2 offers real technical difficulty if the great poetry of this passage is to come through. Equalise both in nuance and speed the slope of quavers shared between the hands. This light murmuring should not be mixed with the 'dolce' melody line which rises in isolation, and whose highest note should be stressed.

From bar 3 (p. 7) Fauré asked me to retain the 'fortissimo' with some warmth, with a diminuendo of course at the end of the passages, but picking up the phrase with more insistence each time.

Bar 3 (p. 8): diminuendo only on the modulation and take note of the progression indicated by the development of the theme in one, then two, then three bars with a 'piano' reprise each time.

Page 9: make the return of the theme very 'cantabile' without any diminuendo until the end of the third bar, to arrive at a gripping 'piano subito'.

To give the necessary amount of relaxation to this charming passage play the triplet 'portando' and stress the bass a little. Take special care not to hurry to the start of the 3/2 time, where again Fauré asked me to play the bass in octaves.

Bar 2 (p.11): at the second bar play the passage with much 'brio', with as much diminuendo as possible. Let the pedal vibrate on the pause but breathing lightly before the repeat of the first melody which returns here "as if from some distant memory". Do not play it fast, with the triplets in octaves very relaxed, the bass line held with the pedal and the arpeggio ascensions without any haste.

The melody should be declaimed fully until the last chromatic ascension, overwhelming because it owes its persuasiveness to a gentleness beyond understanding.

The *Seventh Nocturne* (1897) is more sorrowful, more impassioned, in a word, more romantic than that which precedes. it. Although Fauré kept the same construction, he modified the ending which was no longer entrusted to the initial theme, but that which rises towards the middle of the work. It is its more complex construction which gives this *Nocturne* its character.

This theme is directly linked with the unalterable design of its accompaniment: if they are to be separated, they would lose their meaning. This lengthy lament is interrupted by a melody which is rather timid until it takes flight, but whose surge founders under the weight of the throbbing rhythm of the first theme which returns here. A crescendo of intense expressiveness is followed by a passage of infinite sadness stressed by holding the chords for a long time.

Suddenly, in the treble of the keyboard, a high-pitched note rings out and a lightly balanced phrase follows. This striking contrast serves to bring in the central development until the brutal eruption of a dominating motif in triplets, which turns the *Nocturne* towards its final phrase.

It cuts short its rapture and brings back the first theme in its grief-like shadow until the end where the dreaming theme returns to melt lazily, which rocks in shimmering scales in an atmosphere of mist. So much lyricism and so much modesty can be expressed where restraint is exercised.

The Nocturnes which follow are of less vast proportions. *The Eighth* (1898) is one of his 'short pieces'. It is haloed with the poetry of twilight and the sound of bells.

Ten years passed before the composition of the *Ninth Nocturne* (1908). When the silence of the night spreads its peace on the world, unrequited hearts breathe their melancholy regrets. The harmonic progression which ends here in great rapture is of powerful beauty.

The *Tenth Nocturne* is pervaded with a gentle reminiscence of *La Bonne Chanson*. Fauré wrote the *Nocturne* in 1908 when all his thoughts were absorbed by the composition of *Pénélope*. "The *Nocturne* is just about finished," he wrote on the 15th September 1908. "I hope it will belong to the same family as the nine others. As for *Pénélope*, it has not suffered from this incursion into the world of the piano."

Faithful to the source from which he drew his harmonious equilibrium, the last three *Nocturnes* saw light in 1913, 1915 and 1921. In the evening of his life, in the serenity of thought that is no longer touched with ardour, Fauré found again accents simple, melancholy or resigned, to translate his love of beauty which was still very much alive. His sober, unadorned writing is all the more moving for it. The flame of genius which gave life to his soul dictated to him even in this

Thirteenth Nocturne, op. 117, the pulse of indescribable emotion.

VALSES–CAPRICES

The progression of form in Fauré always showed a superior ability. He could bend the traditional style of writing to the infinitely subtle expression of the most refined feelings, and always respected the demands of pure classical discipline.

Through his astonishing ability for renewal he gave new life to old forms. In his hands the waltz is transformed. Indeed he juxtaposed the word "caprice" which gives its meaning to so much that is new.

"In a world of sound, of resonance and of surging, this feast of the body before our souls offers light and joy." I cannot resist recalling this phrase of Paul Valéry which should be inscribed on the *Fourth Valse-Caprice* which Fauré composed between the years 1883 and 1894. Much more than waltzes for dancing, they are those feasts of the soul of which the poet speaks, the musical feeling which inspires them with the movement which enlivens them in the euphoria born of rhythm linked to the ecstasy of movement. Music and dance: one derives from the other — the primary source of the idea of rhythm, without which the workings of art would remain a dead letter.

Rhythm, the measured flow of time, born with the first beatings of our hearts, remains our surest guide. It is rhythm which gives Fauré's Valses their living warmth. Imagination is given free rein here.

Let us agree with Edgar Allan Poe: "All certainty is in dreaming". It is indeed with dreams that we are dealing here.

Paul Dukas was very fond of the second of these *Valses-Caprices*.

By juxtaposing these words Gabriel Fauré revealed to us the secret of their interpretation.

In waltz tempo it keeps its elegant 3/4 attractiveness. But it is with such charm that he uses the ternary division with its two supports in one bar and its light lift on the second beat.

How very French these waltzes are. It is ages since the waltz lost any memory of its popular origins: Ländler or

Tourdion — what does it matter? German or French? — I don't care. Ever since it was adopted by real musicians the waltz has been at home in the salon and has been welcomed from the start. Mozart and Schubert held to its modest proportions. Chopin glorified it. Fauré made it more capricious yet, a marvellous excuse to refine his writing using all the resources of the piano.

THE IMPROMPTUS

The very intimate attractiveness of the Impromptus is expressed in refined, poetic, often brilliant language. Fauré gave free rein to his thoughts. His inspiration was drawn from the springs of music itself and the emotion that can be heard in them is born of its own beauty.

The *Second Impromptu*, despite its frivolous manner, reveals treasures of great sensitivity. The development of the second theme is enriched by startling modulations, one of the secrets of Fauré's art. I do not consider this the greatest of all Fauré's works as others have claimed. It is a charming work, indeed brilliant, which unlike so many others is quite striking. The structure is delicate. It must be very well played. I know how difficult it is to play it to perfection, but is that a reason not to try...?

From the beginning play the passage in quaver triplets at the same volume despite the fact that the hands alternate. The chords which punctuate it will find their natural accentuation if one does not stress the last two, as one hears only too often.

To lead in the end of the first episode — and its repeats — the movement should be lively so that the passage runs swiftly and lightly. Fauré agreed entirely that one should ignore the marking 'do not hurry' which the printed score nevertheless bears.

The central part is so explicit in itself with its modulations and exalted phrasing that one must shun all excessive lyricism. There is no verbiage here, but a real feeling of warmth which is not to be found in high-spiritedness nor in haste.

Carry lightly the first two notes of the new theme, then play it closely linked with the triplet, without hurry, until the phrase reaches its gentle end. The bass line must be played at equal volume throughout.

This adorable music requires the greatest simplicity of interpretation to make its full effect. A certain amount of 'rubato' is necessary here, as long as all the values are strictly observed. This equilibrium without rigidity is surely the characteristic of all music.

The *Third Impromptu*, written in 1883, is of thoroughbred elegance, full of charm and finesse. It is a delightful little poem. It is built on two themes: the first, lively and supple, rests on a voluble bass line played with childlike dash. The more sensitive argument of the other theme is enlivened with tender and urgent feelings entrusted to the left hand alone, "like a memory", Fauré used to say. Avoid using both hands here which gives it too much weight. Fauré changed the slurs of the left hand in this way (bar 69):

Fauré dedicated to me the *Fourth Impromptu*, written in 1904.

More than twenty years separate these last two Impromptus and the evolution of his musical writing can be discerned here. "My" *Impromptu* belongs to this second creative period, starker and more concentrated still. I was happy and proud to give its première, but I knew from the first that this work would remain the preserve of the initiated.

The *Fifth Impromptu* saw light at Lugano in 1906, between the composition of two scenes of *Pénélope*. At the occasion of our concert for "La Trompette" (a very fashionable chamber music society) we had heard a work of Florent Schmitt in which the theme is in whole tones. The success of this so-called novelty annoyed Fauré, and, furious, he said to us: "I also know how to write in whole tones". He had used this skilful procedure in the *Fourth Impromptu* and indeed in the marvellous ascending passage in the epilogue of the *Seventh Nocturne* in 1898.

He wanted to give further evidence of this in the *Fifth Impromptu*, written in the spirit of a 'moto perpetuo' and whose theme passes from one hand to the other over a delicate network of semiquavers.

When Camille Saint-Saëns heard me play it for the first time in 1909 he was startled by the speed of the passage and its famous whole tone descents which come dangerously close to "throwing the fingers off course", and he said to me after a lengthy silence: "Good Lord, but that's difficult". This was all he said and yet Saint-Saëns was one of the greatest pianists of his time and a close friend of Fauré.

The *Sixth Impromptu* is nothing more than a piano transcription made in 1913 of a rather gentle work written for the harp for the 1903 Competition at the Paris Conservatoire.

A LESSON IN THE PERFORMANCE OF THE *BALLADE*

The tradition of the playing of the *Ballade*, which I have from Gabriel Fauré himself, should not be transmitted by mouth alone. I therefore entrust to this book the task of perpetuating it.

From the beginning one must establish its plan. Although its form is free, one can discern in this work the three classical movements preceded by an introduction. But when I say "plan", it is first and foremost the well-defined outline of the phrase with its form, curves, the colour of its sonorities and the technique it requires.

It is the lack of plan which always gives rise to monotony. While Claude Debussy or Maurice Ravel take special care to indicate the smallest detail, Fauré quite often was imprecise.

The introduction of the *Ballade* is a sort of idealised Nocturne. The accompaniment entrusted to the left hand consists of a series of modulating chords based on a single bass note, sometimes given to the piano, sometimes to pizzicati in the orchestra. The fingering of these chords must be played with care, always putting the theme on the higher note which ensures a homogeneity of sound as long as one does not raise the hand but plays each theme with equal weight.

After a big rallentando on the last chords of the intro-duction, a lengthy pause precedes the exposition of the second idea (letter B[1]) which will often be repeated and developed in the course of the work. The metronome marking of $\bullet$ =76 is closer to the composer's idea than the marking of 'allegretto moderato', which is actually too slow. Above all, this episode should be played with movement and suppleness.

Four bars before letter E relax the end of the passage a little to prepare for the entry of the theme in the orchestra.

So that the dialogue between piano and orchestra, which ends in the splash of sound of the second theme, be played very warmly even when at F the piano is playing alone the character remains that of an ardent lyrical recitative which quietens at the last bar before the andante in 6/8 time whose metronome marking of $\bullet$ =66 should be respected. The pas-sage in semiquaver triplets which comes in answer to the balanced rhythm of the orchestra should be as impalpable "as the breath of a dream", the ternary rhythm of 6/8 adapted to that of the orchestra.

Do not trust the introduction of the marking 'un poco piu mosso', since the music here should correspond with the passage which precedes it. Beat time in two tempi which gives the movement its correct thrust, but I cannot stress too much that this should not be played too fast. Take care that the 'crescendo' at the fourth reprise of the passage be very brilliantly played with the dynamics sustained. Do not forget to pause for breath before the exposition of the third theme which bursts out joyfully.

Fauré wished that the dotted crotchet and the quaver which follows it should both be played without any slur

---

[1] The letters are those of the two-piano score.

between them (the printed score is incorrect) while a few
bars further on the real phrasing is re-established.

At the fifth bar of the *Allegro* one must throw in relief
the notes of the theme shared between the hands, the ara-
besque in semiquavers serving as support in the scale passages
bursting our vividly. The canonic episode vanishes charmingly
and very expressively.

One must give all one's attention to the course of the
crescendo which starts four bars after letter H; it leads in
successive stages to the 'fortissimo' of the next page. Here we
reach the summit of the work where the feeling of enthusiasm
which informs it comes to the surface — but pianists should
watch that the excitement does not modify the rhythm at all.
There is nothing special here except to remember the demands of the text and the need to observe them scrupulously.
Becoming more intense and inflamed, the melody passes
again from one hand to the other. Take care over the
'diminuendo' and pay attention to the sound.

The same applies to the repeat of the third theme which is
shown to best effect with the same vitality. The effusive
cadence which precedes the return of the andante in 6/8 has
a quaver beat. Do not rush the semiquaver triplets so that one
keeps the acceleration for the passage in quaver triplets, and
slow up the advent of the last chromatic notes which should
be played with a feeling for each before stressing the beginning
of the 'allegro molto moderato' which is the finale of this
exquisite *Ballade*.

Fauré preferred that the finale be played in a lively tempo
and in an apposite spirit right up to the change of tempo.
After the cadence of the passage in sixths the slurs of the
thirds require playing of great suppleness, stressing the first
beat on the trill and playing the thirds with a rhythmic
rubato. Playing as fluidly and as poetically as possible, let the
enthusiasm calm down until the peroration, the last passage
repeated with movement.

But God knows, how difficult it is to explain music!

ABOUT 'DOLLY'
Suite for piano, for four hands

One day, with one of his customary express letters, Fauré had invited me to play with him his Suite for four hands, *Dolly*, at the house of Madame Yvonne Sarcey-Brisson, the founder of the 'Annales' and of the admirable work of the Maisons Claires. All the important personalities of the world of art, letters and politics would come to this salon which the charm and intelligence of the hostess made so attractive.

Young Pierre Brisson, wearing an outfit in black velvet with a big lace collar, made a short appearance during the musical hour. The great friendship that I shared with Madame Adolphe Brisson for so many years dates from this meeting. It is thanks to her that I founded the piano courses at the 'Annales' and gave seminars on my musician friends, illustrating their music at the piano.

As Tolstoy wrote in his memoirs: 'If you had to judge everything by reality there would be no fun in it any more". Indeed it was for fun that Fauré led us into this enchanted world of childhood. These short pieces, at once simple and refined, possess a touching grace. Before him only Robert Schumann had been able to penetrate the mystery of the child's soul

Confident of my facts, I set down here again the sources of Fauré's inspiration and put an end to the misleading myth.

Composed between 1893 and 1896, *Dolly* owes its title to the Christian name of the daughter of my friend Madame Bardac. This was the happy lot of this delightful woman for whom in 1892 Fauré had written *La Bonne Chanson* and who ten years later would be the noble companion of Claude Debussy. *Dolly*, who now is Madame de Tinan, was then a little blonde girl of charming behaviour and feminine precocity. The music which Fauré wrote for her is quite in her image. It is the only time that the composer used titles other than those of a musical genre. The album consists of six pieces: in the *Berceuse* one can perceive the musician's feelings in front of such childlike grace. *Miau* is not, as Emile Vuillermoz wrote,[1] the name of the household cat that used

[1] *Gabriel Fauré*

to jump about mischievously, but the nickname that young Dolly gave to her brother Raoul Bardac, who was later himself a pupil of Fauré and Debussy. *Le Jardin de Dolly* is the garden in an enchanted dream, full of perfumed flowers, while *Kitty-Valse* illustrates the whirling leaps of a favourite dog. *Tendresse* makes clear its meaning in its delicate figurations. Finally the *Pas Espagnol* is the transposition in music of the bronze equestrian statue of Frémiet, Fauré's father-in-law, which stood on a mantlepiece in Madame Bardac's house and which was much admired by young Dolly.

"THEME AND VARIATIONS", OP. 73,
composed in 1897

The advice I give here is for experienced pianists. I assume therefore *a priori* that all the musical expressions are familiar to them, as the playing of the piano is concerned as much as the interpretation. I consider it indispensable that one is able to follow my guidance with the music.

This work is one of the most difficult to play satisfactorily, since the character of each variation should be shown to its best account, to the benefit of the whole. The progression in groups should be respected, otherwise it is no longer one work but a suite of separate pieces.

Theme

It is like an Étude, Fauré said, a little paradoxically. We can interpret that through a great simplicity in the exposition with a rigorous precision of the beat. Keep the same accentuation for each note *whatever its value be*. On the last line make the 'crescendo' very expressive. Slow up at the end, letting the C sharp vibrate under the thumb of the right hand to be taken up by the left hand to link it with the first variation.

First Variation

Same movement. The right hand should be very 'piano' and fluid, the left marking the time quite clearly. Watch for the legato which is obtained by changing the fingering on almost each note on the ascending phrase. Fauré changed the dynamics so that the last entry should be more sustained.

The oscillation of the harmony of the second part of the

theme requires more intense playing which relapses into gentleness.

Second Variation

Since the movement grows in steps up till the *Sixth Variation*, one must take care not to shut off too quickly. It needs more spirit than haste. In the manner that Fauré held dear, give the dynamics their precise value. Make sure you observe the crescendo in the second bar, the third loud throughout, and then a short diminuendo. At the third line the melody is emphasised with both hands. Play the fourth more sonorously, then lightly link the last four quavers, holding the C sharp with the fifth finger to its full value and finish very softly. There is a short pause before the *Third Variation*.

Third Variation

Bar 4: on the third beat double the triplet with the left hand, thus:

To give this variation its character one must observe the beat rigorously and in its alternating triplets and twos. Think of Chopin's *Fantaisie* where the same writing occurs. Nothing exasperated Fauré as much as not to hear this cadence observed: one beat of three notes, the other of two. Give the same meaning to the quavers which should be pronounced "like words", without haste.

Generally, the unity should be respected, otherwise the beat becomes unnatural.[1] Give full value to the pedal in C and at the marking 'expressivo' keep to the tempo, play a little more deeply with sustained legato.

---

[1] So as not to spoil the triplet I would generally advise against working on the rhythm of three.

Fourth Variation

There should not be a diminuendo in the preceding bar to lead in the fortissimo of this variation which should be played with great authority and power. Keep the same movement. Take care to keep the fifth finger of the right hand on the upper note.

Never abandon the continuity of the musical phrase; do not cut it as it passes from one hand to the other. The two parts should be independent and yet "overlap". In the second motif take care to link the semiquavers in the bass line and play the small note prettily with the right hand while playing it simply with the thumbs outwards.

Fifth Variation

Do not exaggerate the 'piu mosso' tempo. Pay attention to the "barred" note, which should be heard without breaking the key. Make sure the bass note can always be heard and play the indicated dynamics with dexterity.

When we find the word 'expressif' mentioned for the second time (see *Third Variation*), do not forget the essential importance that Fauré gave to the expression of this episode which he considered one of the peaks of his output. He wanted the first four bars to be played with a very sustained 'piano' so that the crescendo contained thus should finally give life to the rise of that phrase that is repeated twice. Take note of the pause.

Sixth Variation

The fullness of this variation reinvests the theme with all its troubled gravity. Fauré uses here the entire texture of the keyboard. Take care to give the correct sonority to each of the three parts. Let the left hand be heard by giving equal importance to the semiquaver. Here the weight of the hand, without adding to its heaviness, will help you.

The second phrase, very legato, should be played intensely expressively. The magnificence of the theme bursts forth here with unprecedented splendour, whose grandeur and nobility are unparalleled. At the third reprise, while the theme is held in the bass line, play the first note of the sextolets.

Then there is the marvellous link which is made with the low C sharp which is extended to prepare for the 'pianissimo' entry of the following variation.

Seventh Variation

This is the most pathetic in its expressive restraint. An irresistible 'crescendo' accompanies the dialogue between the two hands.

Eighth Variation

"Like a distant organ," Fauré would say. It remains to us to bring it into being. To "gear down" the fingers by constant substitution. This assures equality to the progress of the quavers. The first motif and its repeat should be played as softly as possible; the central part a little more outward — "a dynamic within a dynamic".

This variation is perhaps the most difficult to play. It needs that special Fauré technique which requires so much independence of hand and of fingers.

Ninth Variation

Here we find ourselves in the presence of a profound Nocturne of supreme beauty, when in the second bar the 'pianissimo' G sharp enters and "lights up like a star". It must be preceded with a delicate 'crescendo' of great gentleness.

Fauré asked me to repeat the third and fourth lines, stressing the bass line. The feeling of this passage, amplified by octaves, should be sustained until the 'pianissimo subito' which greets the return of the theme. Take care to keep perfectly equal the descending thirds, punctuated by the call of two chromatic notes shared between thumbs.

Tenth Variation

To give this variation its faultless rhythm, stress the first beat in the left hand and play "voicelessly" the tied notes of the right hand in this same first beat. This gives the feeling of syncopation and ensures the right accent on the chord.

Do not forget that warmth is derived neither from excitement nor from hurrying. To give this passage its mercurial rhythm it must be played without dryness and with the colour Fauré intended. So bear in mind all the dynamics and avoid any weakness, because that is what carries it forward. On the third page (third line) Fauré wanted a very marked accent on the C sharp in the bass because despite the fortissimo indication it is that which marks the start of the phrase which leads to the ending, but he "forbade" me to play the last phrase of the passage in octaves.

Eleventh Variation

The marvellous variation which finishes this work is trans-figured by the key of C sharp major. The melodic beauty of the three voices which weave the counterpoint of this variation is such that one would like to light up each of them and yet "it is their convergence that provokes emotion," as Debussy said of a work of Bach. We must really give of our best to make this music sing.

THE PRÉLUDES

"To clothe thoughts and emotions we need the discipline of form," as Paul Valéry would have it. Without this discipline the creation of music would be no more than a vain "jeu de l'esprit", but to speak of 'jeu' means 'rule', for what is a prelude if not a preface to the whole. The freedom of its structure lends itself to all manner of expression: joyful, as well as sad. In Gabriel Fauré's hands the *Prélude* takes on a thousand facets from which the spirit derives new life.

It was during our stay at Lugano in July 1910 that Fauré finished his *Préludes*. He had confided his grief to my husband at the advance of his deafness. He was contracted to his publisher Heugel to "deliver" each year a certain number of piano pieces. Pressed for time and pre-occupied by his finances, he took up again the suite of *Préludes*, the first three of which had already been published.

On the 27th July 1910, he wrote: "I have finished the *Fifth Prélude* (that's 1,200 Francs earned) and I have begun the *Sixth*. It's sheer misery when I try out what I have written on my marvellous Érard (the firm of Érard used to send him a piano every year), the sounds of the middle range I can just hear in the distance, but accurately, while the bass line and the treble offer me no more than an in-definable din."[1]

In the hope of improving his hearing he left us to take a course of treatment at Ems. He was much worried by the

---

[1] From a private letter.

illness of his father-in-law, the sculptor Frémiet, and he had
to redouble his efforts to be able to continue writing. It was
in these dreadful conditions that on the 5th September 1910
he composed the *Seventh Prélude*

Some months later, Fauré entrusted to me the première of
the Suite of his *Préludes*. This was one of the worst fears
of my life. Too short a period for study in a very busy life
left me worried about my memory, for of course there was
no question of me playing anything other than from memory.
There was a terrible storm that night. Depressed and nervous
I said to my husband: "I am so frightened that I can't stand
upright". "That's not important," he answered "because you
play sitting down". That occasioned a general bout of laughter
in the foyer and I was released from my fear.

Under my fingers the *Préludes* saw the day. What a
shame it is that these charming pieces are hardly ever played
any more.

10 Around the piano

CHAMBER MUSIC

The chamber music of Gabriel Fauré has afforded me my greatest enjoyment:
Two sonatas for violin and piano
Two sonatas for violin and cello
Two piano quartets
Two piano quintets
One piano trio
One string quartet

Modest in number, brilliant in quality, Fauré's repertoire has enriched the heritage of France with its greatest masterpieces. It is we who are responsible for the reputation accorded to Fauré's work. By talking of its charm, its grace, the confidential character of his music, we have given credence to the opinion that Fauré is the master of the half-tint and chiaroscuro.

His chamber music formally gives the lie to this mistaken idea which is, alas, too widely held. Classical in form, it is subjected to the demands of the traditional framework: exposition, development, recapitulation. One should not be fooled by appearances. This "mould" is not rigid: these works are informed with the greatest freedom.

Here as elsewhere, Fauré was a pioneer. He only seems to submit to tradition, as the intrinsic beauty of his themes lends itself to long developments where the music never loses its prerogative. It is with great suppleness that he avails himself of the boldest modulations, returning to the "fold" of the key with out-of-the-way yet certain paths of which he knows the secret. His good taste is his only guide, and it is flawless.

Fauré's *Andantes* are among his most beautiful inventions, lyrical, profound, reflecting grief, resignation and serenity, or even a calm happiness, they evoke echos in us of considerable sensitivity.

His *Scherzi* are petulant in mood, even malicious, revealing a little-known aspect of Fauré's character, but to which some of his letters bear witness.

The *Finales* are superb, radiant with force, power or joy.

Fauré began his work in the field of chamber music with the *First Sonata*, op. 13, in A major, for piano and violin. For a trial effort it is a masterpiece. Nevertheless, there was no French firm that would publish it.

M. de Choudens had given proof of his perceptiveness by sharing with Hartman the publication of the ample harvest of Fauré's first songs, but would not publish this *First Sonata*, written during the summer of 1875 — Fauré was already thirty — in that haven of peace which the affection of his friends M. and Mme Clerc had offered him. It was there, he told me, that he played "the day's writings" as they were written, in front of his friends Messager, Hollman the cellist and the Belgian violinists, Léonard and Ysaÿe, all keen supporters of his work.

On the personal intervention of M. Clerc the Leipzig firm of Breitkopf and Härtel agreed to publish the work, on condition that they became sole proprietors and did not have to spend a penny. What a bitter disappointment for a composer to have to give up his rights for ever, losing any material benefit from his own creation; and what injustice! It was thus that Gabriel Fauré "gave" this first sonata which to-day can be found in the repertoire of all the world's violinists.

Even before the work was first heard in Paris, at the Exposition Universelle of 1878, with Fauré at the piano and a violinist whose name is today forgotten, M. Maurin, Camille Saint-Saëns in 1877, sensing the novelty that this Sonata concealed beneath its youthful features, devoted an article of praise to it.

I often played it with the greatest violinists in the world,

Jacques Thibaud, Georges Enesco, Maurice Hayot and others still, each time renewing my admiration.

The composition of the *First Quintet*, announced as op. 60, was spread over several years and bears witness to the evolution of Fauré's style.

The first *Allegro*, nobly serene, was written towards 1891 between the song cycles *Venise* and *La Bonne Chanson*, the fruitful period of abundant inspiration. Then, having sketched the exposition of the *Andante*, Fauré abandoned it. It lay in his desk drawer until 1903, and it was not until 1904 that the *Finale* was finished with its lively and robust first theme, its graver second subject and its final irresistible enthusiastic rush towards the peroration.

The work was not to appear until 1906, published by Schirmer in New York with the definitive opus number of 89. The *First Quintet* is dedicated to Her Majesty Queen Elizabeth of Belgium.

I am proud to have given the work its first hearing in London in 1910, first in public, then at the house of John Sargent, with the already famous Capet Quartet. It was in the salon of the famous painter that I recognised the lovely sketch, which has been reproduced many times, that Sargent had made of Fauré on the occasion of a visit to London by the master. Fauré's features were fixed in that pensive attitude that was so characteristic of him, his leonine head resting obliquely on the back of his hand. How I longed to have that portrait, and begged Sargent to be kind enough to have a copy made for me.

Some days after my return to Paris I received a carefully wrapped package. It contained the portrait I had wanted, with this note: "I could not find a reproduction and ask you to accept the original, to which I add as accompaniment this water-colour, in the hope that it will please you." I have never in any circumstances wanted to part with one or the other, with one close exception, however. This was when Henry Rabaud, succeeding Fauré as Director of the Conservatoire, in 1920, asked me for permission to reproduce this portrait of Fauré, although the latter had said to him: "You can always ask her, but she is bound to say no". We had fallen out a long time back, it is true, but why would I have refused?

It was with the *First Quartet* that I made one of my debuts playing Fauré in public. It was at the Société Nationale, I was playing with the Capet Quartet and Fauré turned the pages for me. I was considerably excited. How could I resist this vigorous music, burning with life and communicative warmth. At the end of the marvellous *Andante*, the sorrowful echo of the break of Fauré's engagement with Marianne Viardot, I could not keep back my tears. This touched the composer and I still have the letter he wrote to me then, and which so profoundly changed the life of this young musician.

How simply this music is arranged in its respect for the classical norms of form and plan. "The four traditional movements are in their place and obey the rules of academe" his faithful pupil Roger Ducasse told us. "Everything here seems astonishingly simple and clear with a precise sense of balance and above all 'that spiritual perfection of rhythm and proportion'. There is no lapse in this writing, so sure, so skilful, whose mastery is incomparable. There is never any weakness nor fatigue, which would slow down the effort. For Gabriel Fauré the feelings of the heart come before the work of the mind."

How many times have I played this *First Quartet*? I do not know any more. It was sometimes on my own account, sometimes to replace Fauré at short notice. This very human work has found a large audience abroad. The great Soviet artists have begun to play this work since 1955, when I played the *Ballade* for the first time in Moscow. Let me take as example that marvellous recording of the *First Quartet* by the most famous ensemble of the USSR, Gilels, Kogan, Rostropovitch and an excellent violist. How well they knew the breath, the spirit of Fauré in their combined playing. It was with much graciousness and modesty that they submitted their interpretation to me, asking for my instructions on the exactness of tempi and dynamics. It is in gestures of this kind that one recognises the truly great.

Fauré was too secretive about the sources of his inspiration for us to value his rare confidences as anything but priceless.

"It was not just in the *Andante* of the *Second Quartet* [composed in 1886] that I remembered having translated (almost involuntarily) the distant memory of bells which in the evening at Montgauzy — and this is some time ago — came to us from a village called Cadirac when the wind blew from the west. From this dull sound a vague dreaminess arose which, like all vague dreams, is literally untranslatable. Only, does it not happen often that some exterior fact numbs us so that our thoughts become so imprecise that in reality they are not thoughts, and yet are nevertheless something in which we can take pleasure? The desire for things which do not exist perhaps, and this is indeed where music holds sway".[1]

I carry great memories of the recording of the *Second Quartet* of Fauré which I made with my friends Jacques Thibaud, Maurice Vieux and Pierre Fournier. We had played it in public a week beforehand for the Société des Amis de Fauré. Maurice Maréchal had played the cello. It was on the tragic morning of the 10th May 1940 that the recording was due to take place. Bombs had been falling on Paris all night. At eight o'clock I switched on the radio and heard: "M. Frossard [a Minister at the time] is speaking to you." Silence, then: "Holland has been invaded."

Roger Thibaud, Jacques' son, was in the front line in this area. I feared the worst when I went to fetch Jacques Thibaud to go off to the Pathé-Marconi studios in the Rue Albert at the far end of Paris. He already knew the unhappy news.

Overcoming our mortal fear with that courage that artists so need, we started our recording in an extraordinary atmosphere. Never had Thibaud played so well. We were all overwhelmed. Swept up by the music beyond the reach of the present time, we succeeded in the tour de force of recording, without any lapse, the entire Quartet in one day. It was sublime. After the astonishing Quartet, where the piano assumes the leading role, the red light went out and Jacques Thibaud, whose humour had not left him, put his hand in his waistcoat pocket, took a two sous coin from it, put it on the

---

[1] Thibaud. *Private Letters.* Stresa, 1906

piano and said to me: "What you have just done there pays
well, my dear Marguerite." Poor, dear Jacques, he had no
inkling that, two days later on the 12 May, destiny was to
take his son from him.

When, many years later, I played this record to my friend
Gilels, the great Russian pianist, I could not hide my emotion.
He was still enraptured, seeking words to express his feelings,
and finally he said slowly: "That, Madame, is one of life's
great moments."

Age removed Fauré from human considerations. His almost
total deafness isolated him from the world. His thoughts were
then transformed into music where only the essential was left.

The purity of the expression of the *Second Sonata for
piano and violin* has some penetrating moments, sorrowful at
times, but which do not shatter the profound rapture, indeed
full of warmth, which one can always feel beating in the
depths of his old heart.

"I work peacefully at what will be (at least I hope) a second
Sonata which will be dedicated to the Queen of Belgium,
who is a violinist and has shown herself sympathetic to my
music."[1] It was thus that he announced the first sketches
of this Sonata.

The *Allegro* and the *Finale* were finished during the
summer. For the *Andante*, composed in the course of the
next winter, Fauré took up again as his theme that of a
symphony which he had destroyed after a single performance
in 1885 at the Société Nationale. This is music where the soul
becomes melody and which he would announce with the
simple words: "I do not think I will have wasted my time".

The two *Sonatas for piano and cello* reveal wondrous
riches in sound. Here, as in the *Trio*, the writing has become
more aesthetic, but this voluntary bareness reaches true
grandeur.

Finally, the *String Quartet* is his swan-song. All the love
of the world is wrapped up in it. Love, that eternal word,

---

[1] From a private letter, August to September 1916, Évian.

marvellous in that one can say it again and again and it never repeats itself. One can see in this musical testament great resignation, not to say renunciation. With great serenity he seems to face the last moments of a life which he felt ready to leave him.

In the *Allegro* of this Quartet he used again the themes of a violin concerto, written towards 1876 and which, too, was destroyed after he'd had it played at the Société Nationale. Thus, at nearly a half century's distance did Fauré not deny his earlier thoughts. He gave here proof of his fidelity to his Muse and credence to the idea that his evolution is more formal than emotional. He did not escape the common law of the passage of time; youth, maturity, old age, with all the inescapable submission that it entails, just as eternity changes everything. Having known all the anguishes of creation, he allowed himself the musical luxury of contemplating the infinite, because he knew that his message would survive him. He gathered the pulse of joy that lift up the soul at the moment that it prepares to leave the earth, a pulse with which his *String Quartet* is imbued. This was the final detachment from earthly things, the revelation of a peaceful beyond. "As for my work, I can say that it reaches its end" he wrote modestly when he finished his *Quartet*.[1]

Foreseeing his end close at hand, he remained faithful to the discipline he had always imposed on himself by submitting his works to the judgement of his friends and expressed his last wishes thus: "I do not want my Quartet to be published and played before it has been tried out in front of my friends, who have always been the first to hear my works: Dukas, Poujaud, Lalo, de Lallemand. I trust their judgement and it is to them that I leave the decision of whether this Quartet should be published or destroyed." What sublime modesty.

Saint-Saëns had already said of his friend Fauré: "He lacks one fault which for an artist is a quality — ambition".

---

[1] From a private letter.

11 *In paradisum*

Now, as the word 'end' appears from my pen, I must leave you, my dear souvenirs of Fauré, who have enriched my life so much. I have lost all notion of time and reliving them. Your company has led me to the end of the road without bitterness as without pride, without envy as without regret.

The sounds of the divine *Requiem* ring out in my memory. They accompanied Gabriel Fauré on the day of the final farewells at the Madeleine in November 1924. I cannot hear them without our past surging up.

It has been said of the *Requiem* that it is not "Christian" because it lessens the horror of the *Dies Irae* and lights up with eternal hope in its *In Paradisum*. Fauré's genius was in full flight when he composed his *Requiem* in 1887. He was much distressed by the recent death of his father, and, overwhelmed by his first confrontation between life and death, Fauré still did not feel any sense of revolt. The melodies of his *Requiem* are without violence. He did not record terror but a gentle certainty of divine mercy. "If I were God, I would have pity on the heart of man." It is the same credo that Debussy would later put in the mouth of Arkel in *Pelléas et Mélisande*.

Fauré, too, would say: "For me art and music especially consists of raising ourselves as high as possible above that which is." Music, of which he was moulded, is surely the luminous proof of the Divinity.

In this chapter of Truth, before the idea of Death, I owe it to myself to recall the estrangement which occurred in 1912 between Fauré and my household, of which I have never been able to discover the hidden source, unless it was the accumulation of "trifles". He created the most paradoxical of situations, since through my duties as Professor at the Conservatoire I was constantly placed in his company, and yet up till the last day we observed the rule of silence which had put an end to our relationship.

It doubtless needed the intervention of very vigilant enemies to influence Fauré in this way. His heart was not thirsty for fidelity. Can you hold it against him? Is it not better to accept people as they are? Through friends who stayed loyal to both sides I knew that Fauré, too, was not happy with this situation.

On my part I adopted the habit, not without difficulty, of separating my admiration from my resentment. The betrayal of affection was difficult to pardon:

"Heureux qui peut bénir,
Grand qui sait pardonner..."[1]

My husband, perhaps to help support him in his disillusionment, would often repeat this phrase of Victor Hugo. No word of explanation ever occurred between Fauré and me. From one day to the next he stopped coming to sit at our table, where his place was always set.

More than the regrets of the years that have passed, it is the pain he gave my husband that I hold against him. The trust which united them was total. The composer of *Pénélope* called so many times on his friend Jo de Marliave, on the morning that he dropped by at the house asking him to write an article or to help him in some other work. Marliave knew Fauré's work long before he knew the man. He never turned back on his admiration for it. Nothing and nobody could break it. Despite all the vicissitudes of life, my husband never modified his opinion of the work, even when he was disappointed by the man.

After this break, the only material proof of which was the desertion of our hospitality, my husband remained clear and just. The article that he wrote on *Pénélope* is of such sincerity that it merits its place as an appendix in this book.

[1] Happy is he who can bless,
Great who can pardon . . .

The first production of this masterpiece in 1913 in the Théâtre des Champs-Elysées filled my husband with such enthusiasm that Roger Ducasse said to him as they left the hall: "I am sure that if you met Fauré on your way out you wuld have given him your hand." And he replied, looking towards Ducasse with his clear expression: "Without any doubt you can well believe it".

Nonetheless, he had been touched to the depths of his heart by Fauré's incomprehensible attitude. "Well," he said to me, "he is weak and perhaps a little cowardly." These were the excuses he made for him. But he always kept on him two rough copies of letters addressed to Gabriel Fauré "in seach of lost friendship", and which had never received replies. In October 1914 I found them in his portfolio, left behind on the occasion of his departure, alas without return.

On his part, was Fauré at peace with himself? I doubt it, and want no more proof of his regret, perhaps even remorse, than these letters he sent to our mutual friend, a writer to whom Gabriel Fauré had introduced us. One, written at the time of mobilization, says: "I learn that Marliave has left for the army. I hope with all my heart that nothing happens to him." The other, dating from this same August 1914, reveals his apprehension at the announcement of the first bad news which let us all fear the worst.

In 1920 I undertook publication of the book that my husband had written about the Beethoven Quartets and had all the notebooks and documents to hand. The work has just been republished and is still regarded as the authoritative on the subject.[1] It saw the day thanks to the valuable collaboration of my friend Jean Escarra, the distinguished musicologist and Professor at the Faculty of Law, and his brother Édouard, an excellent musician and learned Beethoven enthusiast. Romain Rolland, asking me for permission to quote certain passages in the study that he was writing on Beethoven, said: "It is Marliave who better than any of us understood the soul of this great musician."

---

[1] Juilliard.

And what lovelier tribute can there be than that of Édouard Herriot, writing in the preface to his *Life of Beethoven*: "The work on the Quartets is a living monument of knowledge and love. That such a disciple should have perished one August day in 1914 is not the least gripping proof of the barbarities and atrocious stupidity of war."

For the first publication of this work I asked my friend Roger Ducasse to suggest who could write the preface for it. Without hesitation he said: "But Gabriel Fauré, of course. I am sure he will accept. I shall speak of it to him right away."

Indeed Fauré did accept. It was the loveliest reparation that he could make to the memory of my husband. By signing the preface of these pages that contained the thoughts of Jo de Marliave, I felt that Fauré was answering to himself for his deceitful conduct. Although I wished to avoid any useless meetings, chance put us again on the same path. It was towards the end of spring 1918.

I had fled Paris and its bombardments and had taken refuge at San Salvadour in the Var, in the hotel built through the efforts of the over-famous Sister Candide. I was working there on *Le Tombeau de Couperin* that Maurice Ravel had just written, dedicating each of the pieces he composed to a young hero killed in the war. It is to the memory of Jo de Marliave that the *Toccata* is dedicated. How he would have loved this music, so French in sound that through its dancing rhythms it perpetuates the spirit of our race.

The piano was situated in an immense hall where I felt a little lost, but I was not alone. As I left the piano, some-one said to me: "Do you know who was listening to you? Gabriel Fauré." It was in this way that I learned that the great man in this difficult period was on a concert tour of the hotels, playing four-handed with his companion Madame H. his *Dolly* suite, and accompanying at the piano Félia Litvinne, the famous singer who was then past her best. It was lamentable. No-one, indeed, was in his right place any more.

The next day I went back to the piano, knowing that Fauré was listening hidden in the shadows, and I played his *Ninth Barcarolle*. Better than any vain words, the music between us suddenly took on a moving eloquence.

If our estrangement had pleased some, it had distressed many others. Among these were Fauré's pupils, to whose works I willingly applied myself. Florent Schmitt, with his customary humour, said to me: "You will have to live for two hundred years, dear Marguerite, to be able to play all of us."

The loss of my husband had brought grief to many hearts. Roger Ducasse, much distressed, kept saying: "I will really miss his advice." Among many beautiful chamber music works, this great disciple of Fauré had dedicated to his teacher his *First Piano Quartet*. The Second was being composed when our argument occurred. More than anybody else he felt its uselessness, because he had been witness to the quality of our intimacy. Furthermore, with his characteristic candour, he did not hesitate to offer me, nobly hoping for reparation, the dedication of the *Second Quartet*, saying: "The First is dedicated to Fauré; the Second should be yours by right."

In March 1924 Roger Ducasse brought me the staggering message with which Gabriel Fauré had entrusted him: "I would like to die without leaving any 'scratches' and see Marguerite Long again." And he repeated once again: "No-one has played my music like she has and no-one has written about my music like her husband". In these last moments he wanted to erase the shadows that had tarnished our feelings.

"Come and see him," Roger Ducasse insisted. "He will be waiting for you tomorrow afternoon." It was a Tuesday, I have not forgotten. When I got to his house, my heart beating, I learned that that very day, at five o'clock in the morning Gabriel Fauré had passed away.

I saw him anyway. He lay on his death bed, his features ravaged but still recognisable. This was the last time I saw him, and I cannot say what it meant to me, because Fauré's music was one of my reasons for living, because it was tied to everything that was my musical youth. I shall always remain loyal to it.

For his music I have joined my belief in Fauré with an infinite gentleness, forgiveness, pardon. With it I have rejected the idea of eternal flames and unattainable Paradise. *In Paradisum*.

It is true, as Georges Duhamel wrote in *La Musique Consolatrice*, that "music watches with us among the ruins and ashes of all our former happiness".

Clair Logis
Saint-Jean-Cap-Ferrat, 1963

Appendix

This is the study of Joseph de Marliave, written in 1913,
on *Pénélope* and which Alcan published in 1917

I imagine that the privileged few who, in 1876, were present
at the opening of the Bayreuth Festspielhaus, must have felt,
as in its splendour the work of the great German opened in
front of them, the deep impression of joy, emotion and
enthusiasm which gripped us in the Nouveau Théâtre des
Champs-Elysées that day of the 9th May 1913 when we first
heard *Pénélope*. Moving moments, where one sees, little by
little, page by page, scene by scene, act by act, in an in-
expressible progression, the work take shape, build up and
finally come to life in an atmosphere of clarity and beauty, a
new masterpiece, one of those definitive works representative
of its era and which mark like sparkling lights the infinite
road of art.

It has already been said that since Richard Wagner the lyric
stage has not seen any work which comes as near perfection
as *Pénélope*, nor one which so constantly reaches the heights.
Nothing is truer, but however magnificent the praise it is still
incomplete. What must be added is that for the first time for
more than a century and a half the French *scène lyrique*
has spoken its own language. It was long thought that our
dramatic music had lost clarity of form, simplicity of means,
the exquisite sense of proportion, the intensity of interior
life, the true expression of refined feelings, all those things,
in a word, which are, as G. de Nerval said in his lovely *Sylvie*:
"so naturally French that in listening to them one feels
the best of French life and with the greatest pride and the

greatest emotion." Certainly, for a century and a half we have had great musicians and many among them are the equal of the very greatest, but all of them had undergone more or less foreign influences. One after the other the Glückism, romanticism of German origin and Franckism had stiffened, hardened, mummified the nervous, delicate music, the sober and sparkling lyricism of the 18th century, that art where there has been such a heritage — and since Rameau, in France the Latin genius had fallen silent. The silence has just been broken with the voice of *Pénélope*, and Gabriel Fauré has put another link in the chain that was broken for so long.

None but he, furthermore, was capable today of being the hero of such a worthy mission. He is the purest musician alive today and such as we have possibly never had here. Mozart, Schubert and Chopin alone had to such an eminent degree the divine gift of producing music as spontaneously as a tree produces fruit, and no-one has possessed at the same time such pure craftsmanship.

He is assuredly the greatest musician that our country can boast of and yet showered with honours, glory, fame, Gabriel Fauré was until yesterday not the *least* known, but the most *badly* known in our country. Because he produced above all works of medium dimensions, many thought him to be nothing more than a lesser figure, a 'poeta minor' of music; because he always avoided that grandiloquence which most of Franck's pupils confused with true grandeur; because he is generally happy with moderate means in chamber music he was given the pejorative tag of 'salon musician'. As if the size mattered, or the noise of the music, or the weight of the score, as if in music the content should always be measured by the size of the shell. How many times for so long in my long-lived and still young enthusiasm for Fauré have I revolted against this foolish prejudice? But it came from a powerful source, whose effect on the superficial public — the most numerous, alas — has been undeniable and at present has carried the day. Fauré's exquisite songs and his wonderful chamber music were popular, but only their exterior charm had any effect, and notice was taken only of its extraordinary personal elegance, and the striking quality of his so-called "small-scale" compositions. Deafened by an entire century of Romantic cannon-fire — and of democratic uproar — people were touched neither by the purity of Fauré's art nor by the charm of its incomparable gentleness, nor by the secret force which it possesses to perfection. It was not understood that there was more music in one song of the master, in one of his Nocturnes, Valses or Barcarolles than, say, in such a vast symphony or opera, with or without prologue, that its intolerable duration alone impresses the public. It had not been seen that under their light and charming appearance his compositions, perfect in the rightness of their proportions, expressed with the purest and most intense accents all the feelings that touched the human soul: love, melancholy, joy, sensual pleasure, pity, tenderness and the nostalgia of happiness. The theatre, through the effect it exercises on the spectator, finally gave Fauré the possibility of entering most directly into contact with the audience and the sure and obvious beauty of *Pénélope* finally opened all eyes. It evoked an admiring surprise in all those who until now had been blind to the discreet grandeur of Fauré's music, while for the others who had known and loved the master's music for a long time there was no astonishment, but a peaceful, tranquil joy to see blossom so naturally in a new work the riches of expression, inspiration, of music which they admired in Fauré's work, under the charming veils which enveloped them.

The libretto of M. Fauchois is not without its faults, especially from a literary viewpoint. But that does not matter. It is animated by sincerity and strength of feeling and its lyricism is very profoundly musical. By eliminating all the unimportant episodes from the story of the Odyssey, by centering all the interest around Ulysses and Penelope, the hero of a doubly faithful love, M. Fauchois showed he knew how to build a poem on sober, broad and harmonious lines where the music can pour out freely and whole-heartedly.

The music of *Pénélope* follows the action so closely that you cannot follow one without the other. Let us be careful then not to separate them.

A well developed overture precedes the first act. This is not an independent piece free of the body of the drama, as was formerly the case, nor, as then became the norm, a preface, a résumé of ideas to come, a symphonic poem where the action is summarised. It is a prelude more than an overture. As with Wagner for *Lohengrin*, *Tristan* or *Parsifal*, Fauré took for *Pénélope*, amongst all the motifs of the score, two themes — here they represent the two principal characters — and he has made a symphony from them. Thus all of *Pénélope* is in its prelude like a splash of flowers in a scent bottle. This prelude is of the most touching beauty. The theme of Penelope is heard alone at first, very expressive, with an exquisite grace and painful sadness. It is like a planctus which arises, alternately hopeful and despairing. It seems, in grieving starts, to reach fits and towards the theme of Ulysses. From a distance, at first, in a rustling of strings, then at full volume, occurs the motif of the King of Ithaca, a magnificent theme, a marvellous invention composed of three independent motifs which are combined in a phrase of admirable proportion and rhythm. The first, consisting of two major seconds at an octave interval, sounds like a call, perhaps the fanfare announcing the arrival of Ulysses; the second, rather Wagnerian — the only echo of Wagner in the score — evokes with its double whirl of triplets all the regal majesty of the hero, and the perfect third contains in its striking concision all the certain force which, helped by trickery, will decide the final triumph. One must admire here how Fauré obtains the greatest effect with the subtlest means. This fragment of theme, each appearance of which produces a decisive impression, has only three notes, separated by ascending fifths. Already in *Prométhée* Fauré had written with similar eloquence using an analogous theme — three notes separated by descending fifths — of the sadness and grief of Pandora.

After one of those slow progressions which are characteristic of Fauré, the theme of Ulysses is magnificently declaimed. All is quiet, and the theme of Penelope reappears, sadder here than at the beginning, and moves emploring and weeping after the half-seen husband. Tossed about by the syncopation of the orchestra like the hero on the billows of the sea, fragments of the theme of Ulysses spring up in the symphony, but the regal motif has disappeared. The King of Ithaca is no more than an unhappy man pursued by fate, and when he is to return shortly no-one will recognise him. With an expression of desolation, repeated three times in succession, the motif of the fifths rises like a warning, the volume dies down and the curtain rises.

The stage shows a hall of the palace of Ulysses, leading to the bedroom of Penelope. At the back, curtains conceal an opening through which, when they are drawn back, you will shortly see the countryside and the sea. To the left there is a loom covered by a veil. This occupies Penelope's time. Servants are weaving around her. Some of them, being tired, have dropped their spindles. Serving-girls, dreamy and melancholy, sing of their loneliness in this house without a master which has been visited by sadness. With a weaving rhythm the accompaniment unfolds, adorned with oboe and harp, and draws delicate arabesques which go through delightful modulations. Noisy laughter breaks out behind the stage. A short, ill-tempered theme, both self-willed and fawning, grates in the strings, and the weaving women break off singing. "These are the suitors that our Queen flees," one of them says. In the ten years that have passed without news of Ulysses there are five princes; Eurymachus, Antinous, Leodes, Ctesippus and Pisander, who are waiting for Penelope to choose one of them as a husband and give him the inheritance and power of the king. For ten patient years Penelope has been rejecting them, and the suitors, installed as masters in the old building, drinking the wine of Ulysses and butchering his flocks, console themselves for the Queen's rejection in drunkenness and noisy feasting. But the melancholy serving-girls, weaving their linen in the shade, and seeing these beautiful lords in their embroidered clothes busying themselves around their mistress, do not understand the rigours Penelope must undergo; while each spinner adds anew her charming music to the weft to which is added the theme of the suitors; Melantho, Phylo, Alcander,[1] thinks of the one she would choose if she were Queen. Alas, it is only

---

[1] In the Homeric version of the legend these three are the male-servants called, respectively, *Melantheus*, *Philoteus* and *Alexander*; the first sided with the suitors and was slain by Ulysses, and the other two retainers remained faithful.

a dream and over long sighs of subdued and sad sensuality the spinning woman stops... the spindles are heavy.

Violently throwing aside the drapes which shut off the hall, the suitors arrive. Despite the attempts of the women to stop them, they want to gain access to Penelope's bed chamber and brutally throw aside Euryclea, the nurse of Ulysses, who tries to block their design. The theme of the suitors crawls hatefully on a deep string tremolo, ready to leap up, one might say, on the old servant. It grumbles shiftily, then breaks out; the tumult increases; the perfect fifths of the theme of Ulysses rise from the depths of the orchestra as if, annoyed by the unworthy conduct of the princes, the Gods were at last to produce someone to take revenge. An extraordinary progression of movement and sound is heard and when with the anger of the suitors it arrives at its high point, all this fury stops dead: straight and pure in her dark flowing costume, Penelope has appeared on the threshold.

Never has music weaved around a heroine a halo such as this around Penelope. Dignity, pride, nobility, sad charm, chasteness of manner, and aristocratic modesty under which is hidden a wounded heart shone around the wife of Ulysses and will always be heard around her throughout the vicissitudes of the drama, right up till its end. Penelope reproaches the suitors for their vulgar rage, and while they violently renew their question, she, lost in a dream, hears the voice of her husband telling her to wait. It is an admirable setting and the telling of the dream reaches the point of magnificence in its last phrases. But the Queen's hope seems futile to the suitors. Several years have already passed since Penelope asked them to let her finish, before making her choice, a shroud worthy of the father of Ulysses. The work should be nearly finished, and they are weary of waiting. Their fury breaks out anew when, lifting the cloth which covers it, the Queen shows them the half-woven shroud.

These accounts are in a detached 'parlando', but a 'parlando' where each syllable is equal to the correct note with the inflection corresponding to the most minute requirements of the idea. The declamation seems pure and frank, a living, spontaneous transposition of the word, and above all the music is expressive. Often, during the course of the scene, it expands to take in the form of the song and, like an exquisite flower embroidered on a cloth of gold, one of Fauré's songs is born delightfully effusive.

However Eurymachus has seen maidens playing the flute and dancing across the terrace. He signals to them to approach and then there begins an unutterably charming divertissement. Supported by the harp, the flute plays a supple and pure melody, punctuated every now and then by a discreet cymbal note which is a little reminiscent of *Clair de Lune* and which gives the rhythm of the green-clad dancing girls. This dance is enchanting, alternating with the voluptuous stanzas that the suitors sing each in his turn, it develops without breaking the action. Far from being an accessory, it becomes, on the contrary, an essential part which cannot be separated from the drama, especially at the moment where Penelope, as formerly Alceste, crying over her death during a popular outburst of joy, sings a penetrating lament which is intimately linked with her gracious, almost indifferent, gentleness. It is a magnificent lament, a heart-rending and desperate appeal. This piece is one of the highlights of the score. One must take note of one of the first phrases of the melody. It is below the words: "Master to whom I have given up the treasures of my grace", which outlines for the first time the beautiful love theme which is subsequently to take on capital importance. All of a sudden, from outside, a grievous voice shouts an appeal: "Hola, ho!" In the orchestra the first fragment of the Ulysses theme rustles gently and, covered in rags, his hair and beard in disorder, leaning on a long stick, a beggar appears in the doorway. It is the divine Ulysses. One knows that after the adventures and mistakes which kept him so long from Ithaca, Ulysses, on the advice of Minerva and touched by the Gods with a rod which changed him into an old pauper, made his way towards his dwelling to discover if in this disguise his steward had looked after his affairs well, and Penelope her honour. The suitors greet the old man with great hostility, but when he invokes the name of Ulysses, Penelope interrupts: "Stranger, do not leave, stay in this dwelling." Some chords, some inflections of the voice, that's all there is and yet nothing could express with greater nobility the calm and simple majesty of this greeting.

The feast is being prepared in the neighbouring room; in vain the suitors try to involve Penelope, so they leave her and go off with the serving girls, and the ending of the scene is of extreme sensual charm where the motifs of the stanzas of the spinning women and the suitors are mixed in music of voluptuous warmth.

Only Ulysses, Penelope and old Euryclea are left on the stage. While the latter, on the orders of the Queen, prepares the bath where she will wash the feet of the strange guest, Penelope dreams and sings a moving song built on the love theme and the two themes, heroic and prophetic, of Ulysses.

Suddenly a slow trumpet, pianissimo, breaks the silence with the theme in fifths in, one might say, a new kind of sound. One feels that the pretence of Ulysses has been discovered and that the hero has been recognised. The effect is gripping. Indeed, a shuddering shakes the orchestra. Euryclea starts; on washing the wanderer's leg she has spotted the famous scar which earlier a boar had inflicted on her master while he was hunting in Mount Parnassus. "Yes, it's me, but keep quiet," Ulysses says in her ear, and he leaves with her to partake of the meal which has been prepared for him.

Penelope is alone; fragments of the theme which characterises her are gently passed around the orchestra. Walking silently, the Queen makes sure that no-one is spying on her from behind the tapestry; then, in front of the loom which supports the weft of the shroud, she sits down and thread by thread undoes the work of the day. The orchestral effect here, with harp doubling flute, is charming and picturesque. The suitors have come in on tiptoe while the Queen was working. They surprise her. There is a raucous leap of the suitors' theme, anger, threats... "From tomorrow, o widow of Ulysses, the Priest of Zeus will unite you with one of us. We will not allow you any more delay." They move off vulgarly, while the theme of Ulysses grumbles like a prophetic warning, and Penelope sits, stunned. From this point one should, and right to the end of the act, like Voltaire reading Racine, write throughout: "beautiful, harmonious, sublime". Each bar of the end of this act is full of emotion, each note of the part of Penelope is a tear, the slightest of her words is gentle, but informed with the sadness of death.

Ulysses, still in disguise, and Euryclea who has returned, try in vain to give hope to the Queen. One last time she wants to climb the hill "from where one can see all the divine sea sparkling"; perhaps she will also see the boat of Ulysses appear on the horizon. The beautiful melody is enflamed with immense desire where, with a breath of the infinite, and in its orchestral accompaniment, can be heard mixed with the theme of Ulysses the pastoral theme which will play so great a role in the following act. The Queen, followed by Euryclea, goes back into her bedroom for a moment. Ulysses is alone. He gets up again, goes to the throne of Penelope, kisses the fringes of the drapes which cover it, and the abandoned shroud; and, no longer being able to contain the emotion that wrings his heart, above the excitement in the orchestra, he proclaims his love. This is a sublime moment. The love theme rises wildly, exultantly, full of joy and tenderness. Penelope and Euryclea return; Ulysses has taken on again his humble, stooped attitude. The first notes of the theme, veiled, discreet, arise muted from the quartet like a shy confession. Penelope offers a cloak to the old man and all three walk out into the falling evening, while the smooth outline of the love theme can be heard to rise and then evaporate like a perfume.

The second act takes place in the evening; indeed, it is almost night: the scene is the summit of a hill which overlooks the sea. To the left one can see the huts of the shepherds. A calm moonlight bathes the entire countryside.

At first one can hear distant cries arising and being answered, the calls of the shepherds bringing back their flocks; they set up a sort of rhythm on which a short pastoral prelude scene develops. Alone on the hill old Euryclea dreams before nightfall. Shepherds cross the stage to get back to their home and it is a marvellous countryside, a Poussin in music, of the most serene beauty bathed in a transparent and peaceful atmosphere, on which night spreads its intoxicating charm. Penelope moves forward, followed by Euryclea and some women. Ulysses is with them. Some shepherds are on watch in the distance, sitting round lit fires. There is not much action in the scenes which are to follow, but music loves deeds less than souls, and because of that finds here the opportunity to expand and unfold its action magnificently. There are few acts in all music fuller, more swollen with music than this one. Old Eumeus, his manner simply and touchingly good-hearted, assures the Queen of his faithfulness to the memory of Ulysses and then retires. There begins a long duo between Ulysses and Penelope.

Ulysses is still in disguise, but by allusions and hints predicts the return of the hero that had been thought lost. Penelope, worried and confused, feels an obscure instinct drawing her close to the unknown wanderer. This is a scene which often recalls in its restraint and deep emotion the immortal *Parfum impérissable*; it is a disturbing scene where one feels with each note passion about to break out, and which through its very discretion reaches the peak of feeling. At one moment Ulysses nearly betrays himself when Penelope, desperately calling on her husband, thinks that perhaps he has betrayed the faith that he had sworn to her. The beggar then seeks to calm the Queen down, but his voice trembles with love when the astonished Penelope looks at him and murmurs: "It was the way you said that."

However night has just about fallen. The pastoral theme can be heard again in the orchestra. "We must return" Euryclea says to Penelope. In a sobbing phrase under which, breaking, the love theme can be heard groaning, the Queen bids farewell to the vast sea, to the cruel sea that has not brought back her husband. Yes, rather than put her hand in the hand of one of the suitors, tomorrow she will descend to the realm of Hades. Then the wanderer, to gain a little time, suggests to the Queen to take as husband only he that can draw back the string of Ulysses' bow, a heavy, sturdy weapon which he noticed a little while back hanging in a room in the palace. Penelope, resigned, gives her word, and moves off, and the veiled rumbling in the orchestra spreads on the scene the wonderful calm of the sleeping countryside. There is a long silence, then, very low, two short pulsations, and there follows one of the most moving moments the theatre can produce. All of a sudden, in a swift crescendo, erupt the joy, love, impatience which Ulysses has held back for so long. Standing on the hillock, the King of Ithaca calls the shepherds who are sleeping on the heath and makes himself known to them. He tells them of the revenge that will follow, in a rich aria of Handelian solidity, under which one can sense the accumulation of anger and hatred, and he tells them to come to the palace tomorrow during the feast. The shepherds, kneeling, stretch their arms towards Ulysses and the curtain falls, while in the orchestra, which by a magnificent progression has reached maximum volume, leaps and exults, frenzied, terrible and joyous, the call of Ulysses.

The great hall of the palace at the end of the night: to the right there is a throne on a narrow platform; at the back of the stage there are heavy bronze sliding gates at the top of some steps. They are closed. Dawn appears. Short, muffled chords frame a rapid, angry phrase which slides furtively into unison strings. From this prelude an oppressing, troubled, worried atmosphere reigns. All night long Ulysses, as noiselessly as a shadow, has been wandering about the palace. He has recognised the rooms and found his weapons again. Here is his trusty blade. Vehemently, terribly, he brandishes it, then hides it so that he can find it again when the time comes. Euryclea rejoins her master: Penelope, gloomy and grim, has not slept at all and her silence is terrible. Ulysses reassures her. The muted trumpet plays the theme in fifths with the hatred of the vengeance that is to come. The love theme arises with a radiant smile when Ulysses promises Euryclea that this night she will see Penelope smile. Then Eumeus arrives, the shepherds are ready. They will rush in at a signal from the King. The old man's speech is angry and blunt. One senses in it trickery and hate. Eumeus leaves. The bronze gates slide back in their grooves. We can see at the foot of a southern landscape white rocks, red soil and black cypresses. Daylight floats into the room, and one by one the suitors arrive. A breath of pure air laden with the perfumes of the morning comes in with them. A supple descending violin passage is punctuated with clear harp chords. Antinous, his forehead garlanded with flowers, sings an exquisite song of sighs: "How pleasant it is to be young when the day is so clear!", a moment of tender, singing, light sensuality and so delightful that in all of Fauré's output it is difficult to find anything that can be compared with it.

But deathly forebodings have frightened the suitors. They need wine to drown their fears. Servants bring tables, and while the princes drink, the flute maidens and young dancing girls come to charm them. The cadences of this dance are supple, undulating, caressing, coloured — no, shaded — with an original and discreet orientalism. The entrance of Penelope interrupts them; the Queen is so beautiful and so sad that the suitors, despite their insolence, bow before the majesty of her grief, and Antinous, genuinely moved, asks her in the name of them all to choose a husband from among them, according to her promise. This is a charming madrigal of insinuating yet virile grace which is so typical of Fauré. Under this declamation, exquisitely elegant, the raucous, crude theme of the suitors becomes supple and smiling.

As the beggar has advised her, Penelope states the condition of her choice. She will be the wife only to him who can draw the huge bow of Ulysses. The weapon is brought and the prophetic theme of fifths bursts out, seeming to follow the curve of the bow itself. The suitors draw near. Raised up on her throne, Penelope, sobbing, sees in a vision the anger of the Gods ready to burst on the princes. The atmosphere of the beginning, full of trouble and terror, weighs heavily on the scene which follows. Each prince tries in turn to draw back the string, but all their efforts are in vain. A combination of themes in the orchestra expresses all the rage of the suitors as they are defeated by the trickery of Ulysses. Out of breath, and their hands hurt, they look around uneasily. At the foot of the stage, ready to pounce, the shepherds are grouping silently. Once already Eurymachus has dispersed them. When the princes have given up, the beggar steps forward humbly: "In times gone by people used to boast of my strength and my dexterity. If you will allow, princes, I shall try to shoot an arrow into the yard."

The suitors' theme grates. "What insolence," they say. But Ulysses has gone up to the bow and picked it up. It is a touching moment. The orchestra proudly proclaims the theme of Ulysses. The hero has at last discovered his personality. It is no longer the poor wanderer who holds the terrible weapon in his hands, it is the triumphant King of Ithaca.

Without any effort he draws back the bow string. The arrow whistles, the ragged tunic has fallen half open, and by the armour which it covered all recognise the avenger. It is a signal: the shepherds rush in: Eurymachus and Pisander have already fallen to Ulysses' arrow and sword; the others flee. Ulysses rushes after them and the combat continues outside. The great bronze gate has been closed. The noise gradually ceases. "If he was dead..." Penelope groans. The suitors' theme can be heard like a question, then the beginning of the theme of anger, and finally the gate opens. Ulysses, triumphant, appears on the steps, and Penelope cries aloud.

Then begins the marvellous finale, whose radiant splendour no words can describe. Ulysses and Penelope, in each other's arms, sing of their love that nothing could overcome. Exalted, transfigured, all the themes of Ulysses reappear. The call of the King rings out proudly. The heroic theme of the husband is melted by tenderness. The theme in fifths, sure of itself, rises in the calm joy of the prophecy that has finally been realised. Then, while the shepherds and servants on their knees glorify Zeus who has permitted the victory of the master, the love theme gently soars up in a broader tempo, in one of those vast and slow progressions in which Fauré takes pleasure and which are full of musical feeling. It rises, supported by a flood of constantly renewed harmonies, it rises still without shouts, without bursts of sound, but with a calm and irresistible power, to an apotheosis of sublime grandeur, tenderness and serenity.

Thus is this work a pure masterpiece, and one of the most perfect models of music theatre that we know. It does not embody however, dramatically speaking, any new form, but we would have to go back to the most beautiful examples of dramatic art (*Castor et Pollux*, *The Magic Flute*, *Fidelio*, *Parsifal*, which, too, contain neither system nor formula) to find to such an eminent degree the qualities which are characteristic of it. The balance of its proportions, the constant regard for truth, the intimate union between word and note, the study of the soul, the simple and sublime expression of passion and great feeling, the eloquent orchestra, the interesting harmonies...

The proportions of no other opera are more harmonious,

and not only its external proportions, but internal, which are controlled by the interior structure of the work and which alone give it true grandeur. Penelope and Ulysses, the heroic couple, are in this lyric poem like the classical statue of Athene in the Parthenon, where all the art of proportion that the master craftsmen of ancient Greece possessed was employed only to show it to best account.

There are few dramas that trace in music characters so faithful and so true to themselves, and this is one of the most astounding beauties of the score. With an admirable psychological aptness the music characterises each individual through some essential feature, and follows it with certain precision throughout all its adventures. Throughout the work the greatest effect is obtained with the smallest means, the music springing from each situation. An infallible sense of the apposite brings the themes, few in number but astonishingly expressive, to those places where they are required to comment. The perfection of Fauré's writing is well known and its elegance and solidity are without equal. It may well be the supple and tight counterpoint of *La Bonne Chanson* which gives the harmonic weft of *Pénélope*, but with that stark sobriety which could already be heard in *Promethée* and had established itself in *La Chanson d'Ève*. The orchestral colouring has become clearer yet and shows each section to advantage. The harmonies are strange, conceived with modern freedom and independence but with supreme logic and astonishing purity.

The orchestra, its sounds gentle and finely savoured, is full, colourful, powerful. The quartet plays an essential role which fits perfectly with the subject of the poem. In a tragedy of spirits such as *Pénélope*, an orchestra of sparkling, gleaming, oriental effects would have been out of place, but whenever Fauré finds the opportunity in his path he never neglects any of those picturesque touches which support and command attention. Must we quote examples? The vaporous harmonies of the cloth which hides the loom at the moment when it is raised; the strange effect already quoted when Penelope tears out the threads she has woven, the exquisite charm of the rustling of harps in the second act when Penelope carries in the flowers she has gathered, and the sinister cawing of the crows, and the strange groans of the bow which the suitors try to draw... Moreover, the orchestra has a sensitivity and suppleness equal to that of the vocal parts. With astonishing mastery, Gabriel Fauré has succeeded in expressing, using variations in sonority, the finest nuances of feeling. I have already quoted all the expressions of anger, joy, vengeance that a simple change in sonority allows the theme in fifths to assume. Let us quote one last example: notice in the first act, during the voluptuous stanzas sung by the suitors, the way in which the clear, light chords of the harp suddenly become heavy and spread out as if to underline the insistent loutishness of Ctesippus, insulting the queen of his desire. But the most admirable and rarest thing in *Pénélope* is that 'odor di musica' which rises ceaselessly from the first to the last note of the score.

It is the inexhaustible richness and constantly renewed outpourings of this music — and has yet a sobriety which through some miracle is joined with this abundance. Under an ancient portrait of Glück can be read this legend: "He preferred the Muses to the Sirens." Fauré, a purer musician than the composer of the *Iphigénie* operas, showed in *Pénélope* that he could unite in harmony the voluptuous Sirens with the serious Muses of order and intelligence. So much music and so wonderful, not a useless bar, not a note more or less than is required; much substance yet little material: it was the craftsmanship of Mozart just as that of Fauré, and this simplicity which excludes dryness is so great that it can surprise us before it touches and moves us.